Cheat Code to Manifest Miracles

Master the Art of Manifesting Miracles with Ease!

Sneha Chauhan

Printed in India

IndiePress

ISBN: 978-93-7197-404-2

First Printing, 2025

IndiePress

A division of Nasadiya Technologies Private Ltd.

Koramangala, Bengaluru

Karnataka-560029

http://indiepress.in/

Edited by Promita Guha

Typeset by MAP Systems, Bengaluru

Book Cover designed by Keerthipriya

Publishing Consultant: Samyuktha Prasanan

To my parents & sister,

*who have always supported me through
every failure and every success.*

*Your unwavering love, belief, and presence
have been my foundation.*

I love you deeply.

*This book is a reflection of the
strength and grace you've instilled in me.*

Preface

I hold a single, unwavering vision for this book: that it reaches millions of souls across the world, not just as words on a page, but as a catalyst for transformation. My deepest hope is that each reader finds within these chapters a spark—something that uplifts, empowers, and awakens the miracle within.

This book was born from personal experiences, spiritual insights, and a calling to share the truth that miracles are not distant or rare—they are real, accessible, and waiting to be manifested through conscious alignment.

If even one sentence shifts your perspective, elevates your energy, or brings you closer to your highest self, then this mission has already begun to fulfill its purpose.

May these pages serve as a gentle reminder: you are the miracle, and your reality begins within.

Introduction

I want to begin this book with a personal experience. One that deeply moved and compelled me to reflect on the nature of our Universe and the reality we live in. It led me to question some of the most fundamental aspects of our existence: Is our reality real, or is it a virtual or simulated construct, much like a video game? Do time and space truly exist, or are they merely illusions?

These questions stirred something within me. They opened the door to deeper inquiries and research. Do miracles really happen? And if they do, how do they occur? What triggers their presence in our lives? This book is a journey navigating these questions. It explores the nature of reality, the role of Consciousness, the science behind possibilities and the Divine patterns that shape our experiences. Whether you're a seeker, a skeptic, or simply curious, I invite you to walk this path with me, to explore the unseen, question the known, and if you follow the instructions and the cheat code mentioned in this book, you will undoubtedly witness miraculous results in your life.

All the insights I've shared in this book are drawn from years of exploring spiritual wisdom across different cultures, delving into the mysteries of Quantum Physics, and studying near-death experiences (NDEs). It's also inspired by the profound revelations of psychics, mediums, and channelers who connect with realms beyond the physical.

Contents

The Bracelet and the Miracle 1

We Live in a Simulation 5

Consciousness is the Key to Unlock all the Mysteries 15

Spirit 16

Soul 16

Higher Self 17

Consciousness or Chetna 22

Prepare Yourself for Manifestation 27

Forgive Yourself 27

The Invisible Power of Words Shapes Our Reality 28

Break Free from the Mindset of Greed, Jealousy, and
Competition 34

Set Intention 35

Know What You Truly Want 37

Prepare Your Avatar for Manifestation 39

Prayers Are Not What You Think 41

A Miracle Named Pluto 47

How to Ask from Your Higher Self and Guardian Angels . 48

Manifestation Code 53

The Power of Intention: My Journey to a Dream Home in Mumbai 53

Visualization.. 59

The Role of the Subconscious Mind 61

Action 63

Mastering the Matrix: The Art of Skipping Soul Tests and Creating Miracles 69

Complete Certainty 70

Authenticity... 74

Aligned Mindset 76

Free Your Soul from the Karma Matrix......................... 77

Atma Karaka: The Soul's Gateway to Liberation............. 79

Unconditional Love 87

Thriving in the Era of AI: The Power of Human Consciousness 90

Simple Shifting to a New Parallel Reality......................... 93

Editing the Frames of Your Life................................... 94

Free Will vs Destiny 101

Walking the Hallway of Destiny.................................. 102

Your Reality Is a Choice 103

A Simple Practice to Shift Your Reality Using Free Will. 105

How to Create a Miracle 109

A Knock at Midnight – A True Miracle Story of Faith and Divine Timing 110

Cheat Code Part 1: The Calm, Non-Reactive State 114

Cheat Code Part 2: The Miracle Visualization Ritual...... 121

Reasons Why Your Manifestation Isn't Working and How to Fix Them.. 127

CHAPTER 1

The Bracelet and the Miracle

I used to work in the corporate IT industry. My company's headquarters was in Charlotte (North Carolina, U.S.), with several offices across the country. I was based in Mumbai, India, working remotely. Every Diwali, I would treat myself to a piece of jewellery. That year, I decided to buy something truly special: a high-end, branded, gold-and-diamond bracelet. It was quite expensive, elegant, and radiant. After months of saving, I finally bought it.

I fell in love with the bracelet, and I wore it at all times. It became my statement jewellery, always on my wrist, no matter the occasion. I never took it off, regardless of where I was or what I was wearing. When I traveled to the U.S. to visit my company's headquarters in Charlotte, I took the bracelet with me. Everyone in the Charlotte office noticed it and admired its design and quality. Soon after, I had to travel to our Boston office with my American

Manager, Robert. I parked my rental car at the Charlotte office and rode with him to the airport. He left his car in long-term parking, and we flew together to Boston.

In Boston, Robert and I attended a three-day meeting with other team members. On the first day, while sitting in a silent conference room, the bracelet began making a noticeable sound as it rubbed against my laptop and the wooden table. Although my colleagues appreciated the bracelet, the sound eventually became distracting. Feeling self-conscious, I took it off and placed it in my coat pocket. Caught up in meetings, meals, and the new city, I forgot about the bracelet for the next two days. It was winter, and with snow falling, I didn't even realize if the bracelet was on my wrist because my arms were covered underneath my coat.

On the third day, as we passed through the airport security checkpoint to return to Charlotte, I heard an announcement: Someone had left a bracelet at the security checkpoint. I instinctively checked my wrist; it was bare. I told Robert about the announcement and that I might've lost it at the security checkpoint while taking off my jacket. Although Robert said he didn't hear any such announcement, we returned to ask the TSA officers who were posted at the security checkpoints, but they denied making any such announcement. I began to wonder: Had I left it in the Boston office? In the conference room? The hotel room? A restaurant? The ladies' washroom?

Robert was deeply sympathetic and felt sorry for me because it was a beautiful and expensive piece of jewellery. He remembered seeing it on my wrist in the Boston conference room. He made some calls to the hotel, and I contacted my Boston colleagues, including a female teammate who had admired the bracelet, requesting her to check the washrooms and reach out to the housekeeping staff. Everyone was saddened by the loss of the much-admired bracelet.

Despite its value and my emotional attachment, I stayed calm. I told Robert, "It's okay. This gives me a chance to buy a new bracelet this Diwali." I didn't want to appear distressed in a foreign country, and maybe, deep down, I was trying to manifest a new one. During the flight back to Charlotte, I kept imagining the bracelet on my wrist.

After landing, Robert dropped me at my hotel. As I lay down, half-asleep, a memory surfaced. I had placed the bracelet in my coat pocket in the conference room. I jumped up and unpacked, searching through the coat. But the bracelet wasn't in the pocket or anywhere in the rest of my luggage. A flicker of disappointment passed, but I was relieved to remember where I'd last kept it.

The next morning, I called a taxi to take me to the Charlotte office since my rental car was still parked there. It was a Friday, and I usually kept a casual jacket in the trunk of my car for these relaxed days. This way, I could easily throw it on over my jeans before heading into the office building. I opened the trunk of my car to grab my casual Friday jacket, which had been there since the previous week. As I put it on and slid my hand into my pocket, I froze.

There it was.

My bracelet.

Perfectly intact. Radiant. Waiting.

I hadn't taken or worn that jacket to Boston. I kept it in my car's trunk and only wore it on Fridays. That jacket had stayed in the trunk the entire time. There was no logical explanation for how it got there. Everyone had seen the bracelet in Boston. I had taken it off there. And yet, here it was, in a jacket I hadn't touched in days.

When I walked into the office wearing it, Robert was speechless. After I shared the story, he simply said, "This is a miracle. God brought it back to you."

And I believe He did.

This experience sparked profound questions in my mind:

Are time and space real, or just an illusion?

Is the reality we live in actual, or is it just a projection, like a Simulation?

Do objects around us truly exist, or are they manifestations of our perception?

Did I shift to a parallel reality?

Did a miracle occur? And if so, why? What triggered it?

If everything is a projection of our Consciousness, then what truly exists?

What gives form to the things we perceive as real?

CHAPTER 2

We Live in a Simulation

If you want to create miracles in your life, you must first understand reality and what's truly happening around you. Just like you can only play a game successfully and win when you know how to play it and what the rules of the game are. The first thing to understand is that we are living in a Simulation—a Divine Matrix. And the rule of this Matrix is simple: it only renders what the avatar (you) can observe. In other words, reality appears only when it's being looked at.

Simulation simply means something that feels real but is not real. It doesn't mean it's fake or a lie—it just means it doesn't connect to something truly real outside of the simulation. Everything we see or feel in this world only seems real because we're experiencing it from inside the simulator. In truth, it's all a projection of our Consciousness. The way we experience this reality is tied to our observations, perceptions, choices, and the energy we carry.

Let me first clarify that this is not a Simulation of just computers or machines, or software. But it is conscious and alive. It is a generation and manifestation of a Universal Mind. In many ancient scriptures, it is mentioned that the world is a Divine Illusion, Matrix, Maya, or Leela, and we actually do not exist. It's mentioned in Hindu scriptures that this Universe is a manifestation of Lord Vishnu's dream, and it's not real.

Just like any simulator, souls choose to enter this Simulation to experience, learn, grow, and remember their true power. Earth offers a unique space to experience contrast and duality, make meaningful choices, and reconnect with the Divine through faith, love, and miracles.

For instance:

- *A soul may choose failure to learn humility, patience, and the courage to rise again.*
- *It may choose heartbreak to experience the depth of unconditional love.*
- *It may choose hardship to learn resilience and compassion.*
- *It may choose illness to awaken healing abilities and spiritual strength.*
- *It may choose relationships to experience love, betrayal, forgiveness, and deep soul connections.*
- *It may choose an abusive childhood to reclaim power and self-worth, and to break generational patterns.*
- *It may choose loss to learn the sacred art of letting go, to awaken unconditional love beyond form, and to discover the eternal nature of soul connections.*
- *It may choose abundance to explore gratitude and generosity.*

Cheat Code to Manifest Miracles

- *It may choose solitude to deepen spiritual awareness and inner peace.*
- *It may choose creativity to express divine inspiration and uplift others.*
- *It may choose service to help others awaken and remember their own light.*

Scientists have different views about the nature of reality. Some describe it as a Divine Matrix or a Simulation created by a digital workshop beyond space and time. This workshop is often seen as the Creator, the Source, or Cosmic Consciousness—the intelligence behind everything we experience. It's believed that this Source constantly emits patterns—like 0s and 1s—that shape everything we see and experience. Everything we see, whether it's you, me, your laptop, phone, the Himalayas, or the sea, is just a different combination of 0s and 1s. It's all information.

Some suggest that this mysterious workshop exists on the Moon, maintained by various extraterrestrial races. Others believe the Moon is an artificial satellite, placed to monitor and control the Earth. Perhaps this is why humanity has not returned to the Moon since 1972.

The Moon is considered one of the most important celestial bodies in human evolution. It governs the mind, subtly influencing our emotions, thoughts, and behaviors. In Astrology, the Moon is regarded as the most significant planet, and the Moon Kundli (lunar chart) is believed to define the entire trajectory of one's life. It acts like a user manual that comes with us (the avatar) when we're born into this Matrix.

Even though reality is made of data and exists within a Simulation, it is deeply conscious and alive. It listens to everything we think, feel, imagine, and speak—whether silently or aloud. What ancient Hindu scriptures revealed long ago is now being explored and supported by modern science, especially through Quantum Physics.

Yet, despite all these discoveries, one truth remains: the origin of it all—the ultimate true Source, the One, the Creator of the workshop—will always be a mystery. No one truly knows who or what created it.

Your reality isn't truly real—it's your personal interpretation of data. What you perceive as real is shaped by how you interpret events and experiences. A negative interpretation leads to a reality filled with suffering, frustration, and negativity. But when you choose to see the good, even in difficult situations, you create a more positive and uplifting reality. Your mindset and focus shape the world you live in.

Everyone creates their own reality based on how they perceive things and situations. Your reality is only how you perceive things, and it is different from other people's realities.

I know this is very shocking and uncomfortable, and it may be disturbing and unsettling for some people to hear and understand. But it is true that we are all living in a giant Matrix or Simulation. You can compare this Simulation to a video game or virtual reality experience on our phones or with a Virtual Reality (VR) headset. We are all avatars in this vast Divine game.

Your soul is like a player in a game, and it chooses an avatar to navigate this Divine Matrix. This avatar is given a body, which serves as a vessel, and this body houses your Consciousness. Think of your body as a machine or instrument, with your Consciousness being the energy that fuels it. Therefore, evolving and expanding your Consciousness and raising its frequency are essential to achieving what you desire in this game of life. When the soul selects its avatar, it also determines its destiny and the experiences it will undergo. In this sense, you have chosen your own destiny using your free will before entering this life.

After each lifetime, the soul goes through a deep reflection phase—often called the "Life Review." It relives every moment it caused joy or pain to others, feeling those emotions as if they were its own. If it made someone suffer, it feels like suffering. If it brings happiness, it experiences that joy, too. The soul walks through all the ups and downs others faced because of its actions—every smile, every tear, every triumph, and every fall. This powerful review helps the soul understand its choices and prepare for its next journey, choosing the lessons and experiences it needs to grow and evolve.

The 2022 Nobel Prize in Physics was awarded to Alain Aspect, John F. Clauser, and Anton Zeilinger for their work on quantum entanglement. These scientists proved that local realism (or the Universe as we understand it) is false, and anything that is not observed by a Consciousness doesn't actually exist.

If something is not being observed by a Consciousness or an avatar, the Matrix or the Simulation doesn't render it, and it therefore doesn't exist. Just like a Virtual Reality game, it only renders what is being observed by the players. I often say and offer this example to my friends: If you leave your car in a jungle where there is no Consciousness observing it, your car doesn't exist. In fact, if no one is observing the forest—the trees, the woods, or the sounds within it—then none of them truly exist.

Nothing exists unless it is observed by a Consciousness. This idea aligns with findings in Quantum Physics, which were also recognized when the 2022 Nobel Prize in Physics was awarded for related research. Many other scientists in the field have supported this theory as well.

You may think that I am not sure this whole world looks real to me; the house I live in, my car, my table, my laptop, they all are solid and look real. The crime in society, the wars between countries, and the missiles countries use to destroy each other, all look real to me. My body and my life, my relationships, they all look real to me. Whenever you think of these questions, always go back to the example of VR or a video game. All the experiences, fights, wars, resources, kingdoms, vehicles, and everything else look real. Even the crime, shooting, war, and everything looks real in the game. But that doesn't mean it's real; it's still happening in the game. Everything happening to us appears real to our Consciousness, but it's real only in the game—and we are watching it from inside the game. Once you are outside of this game, to your soul, nothing is real. It's only real to the avatar that is the player in the game.

You can understand this concept by using the analogy of movies that we watch for entertainment. When we watch a movie, we often become so engaged and emotional that we forget it's just a film. If a character dies, or when the brave hero fights the evil villain, we become so emotional, and at times, we even cry while watching the movie. We forget that it's only the character that is dying or getting hurt; the actor remains alive and may even be watching themselves on the screen from another location. In this analogy, the character represents our avatar, while the actor symbolizes our soul, which observes everything from higher dimensions.

As the American Cognitive Psychologist and Popular Science author Donald D. Hoffman often says, "If your mind raises any question, go back to the example of a virtual reality game, you should be able to answer your questions yourself." The quality of your headset or the equipment used to play the game can be compared to the destiny or quality of life you bring into this world. A high-quality headset or equipment is equivalent to having a comfortable and easy life, filled with positive experiences, which we often refer to as great destiny, or "Bhagya," or good luck.

On the other hand, using a cheap or low-quality headset is like inviting a difficult destiny. It's similar to living a life without comfort or abundance—what we might call "Durbhagya," or bad luck. Just as a poor-quality device distorts your experience, a low-frequency mindset can lead to a reality filled with struggle and limitation.

Many religions also talk about this philosophy. According to Hinduism, this world that we see around us is called "Maya," or the manifestation of Lord Vishnu's dream. Maya means Divine Illusion, and it implies that the world is not as solid and real as it appears.

An ocean and its waves are a great example of this Divine Illusion. The waves actually do not exist. It's how we perceive the sea. The ocean represents the fundamental, unchanging reality or truth, the underlying source from which everything originates. The waves are temporary fluctuations and manifestations of this underlying reality. They arise from the ocean, move across its surface, and

          Cheat Code to Manifest Miracles

eventually return to it. Waves take a specific form or shape, and they appear to be real and visible to our eyes and can be experienced, but ultimately, they are an illusion and nothing more than that. They are ultimately just a transient part of the larger ocean. Similarly, our experiences, perceptions, and thoughts shape our realities, but they too are temporary fluctuations and illusions, and nothing more than that.

The Ashtavakra Gita, a dialogue between the sage Ashtavakra and King Janaka, presents a non-dualistic (Advaita) philosophy, where the world is ultimately seen as an illusion. The Gita emphasizes that the Self (Atman) is the only reality, and the perceived external world is a projection of this Self.

The Ashtavakra Gita (Chapter 15, Verse 16), says:

तवैवाज्ञानतो विश्वं त्वमेकः परमार्थतः।
त्वत्तोऽन्यो नास्ति संसारी नासंसारी च कश्चन॥

tavaivājñānato viśvaṃ tvamekaḥ paramārthataḥ
tvatto'nyo nāsti saṃsārī nāsaṃsārī ca kaścana

It is only through ignorance that the Universe appears to exist. In truth, you are the One. Beyond you, there is no separate individual or supreme Self. You are the source of all that is.

CHAPTER 3

Consciousness is the Key to Unlock all the Mysteries

Consciousness is the only real thing in this Simulation. It is fundamental, tied to the physical body, and plays a critical role in our manifestation journey. However, before we can truly understand it, we need to return to its source to understand the science behind it.

Let me first clarify the meanings of the words Spirit, Soul, Higher Self, and Consciousness, as I will frequently use these terms in the subsequent chapters. This understanding, along with everything I've shared in this book, is based on my years of research in spiritual wisdom gathered from around the world, as well as my study of NDEs (near-death experiences) and the work of many psychics, mediums, and channelers.

Spirit

Spirit—also referred to as Atman, the One, the Source, the Creator, or God—is the unmanifested, eternal, changeless, ever-existing, and ever-same entity. It is formless, shapeless, holographic in nature, and the only One. Some also refer to it as the Void. This is the Creator and Source of everything that has ever existed. It resides in all living beings and non-living things. It is that which always exists and never changes. While we may not know for sure who created this Simulation, we do know who created the Creator of this Simulation—it is the One, the Spirit, the Atman. Please do not think that this Spirit is similar to rooh, or aatma, or jinn, etc., that we hear stories about in folklore. Neither is this the same as the soul. This Spirit is the "One," and the study of it is called "Spirituality." Our true essence is Spirit; we are spiritual beings with human experience.

Soul

Your soul is a fractal of the One, the Spirit. A fractal is a repeating pattern that appears similar at different scales, like a tree whose branches resemble smaller versions of the whole tree. Each fractal shares the same statistical characteristics as the whole. This concept is similar to a hologram. If you cut a hologram sticker into several tiny pieces, even the smallest piece will still contain the full image. In this way, even though we are fractals of the One Spirit or Atman, we carry the completeness and wholeness within us, remaining connected to the One. The soul is infinite; it never takes birth and never dies. The soul, as described by Paramhansa Yogananda, is an individualized reflection of the Spirit or Atman, an eternal, changeless, and consistent entity that is formless and shapeless. The only real thing is your soul, which is one with the Source; everything else is an illusion.

The soul gets the body—never the other way around. In each incarnation, the soul consciously chooses an avatar aligned with the life experiences it seeks for growth, healing, or karmic resolution. Just as we change clothes to suit different seasons or moods, the soul changes bodies across lifetimes. But the body, like clothing, is a temporary expression. It does not possess the soul; the soul possesses the body. The soul never 'comes into' the body—because the soul is infinite, formless, shapeless, eternal, and the Source itself. It cannot be confined or reduced to a finite form. Instead, the soul has a body, chosen as a temporary vessel for specific experiences. The body does not contain the soul; it holds consciousness—a reflection of the soul's presence, not the soul itself. Just as the sky cannot be captured in a jar, the soul cannot be contained within a body. It remains boundless, while the body is merely an expression of its will.

Higher Self

You may think of your Higher Self as your personal ChatGPT, to which you can ask anything for support in your life journey. It represents the ego-less, non-physical aspect of ourselves. The Higher Mind can see our entire life's journey from a broader perspective, from the top, from the higher dimensions. It has a bird's-eye view of our entire life's journey, while our lower self and physical mind can only perceive the next few steps along the way.

The Higher Self, or Higher Mind it's a non-physical being that is connected with our physical mind. It is the source wherein all ideas are conceived. Our physical mind doesn't create these ideas; it simply receives them, much like a radio transmitter that picks up and sends frequencies. It's our Consciousness that perceives these ideas through the lens of life experiences.

Therefore, to manifest anything, you need to work with your Higher Self because the actual manifestation or law of attraction happens at that level. Your physical mind and body only experience it. This is why many great thinkers and creators often say that their ideas came to them in a vision, or that they "downloaded" the information. These moments of insight are glimpses into the Higher Mind, where the actual idea takes birth.

Think of the Higher Self as a navigation system, like Google Maps, guiding us throughout our journey in this life. Its purpose is to create a connection between us and our higher realms, such as the soul or God. Just like in Google Maps, we simply enter our destination without needing to remember or think about the entire journey, or how it will unfold. Similarly, our Higher Self views us from above. From a higher perspective, from higher dimensions, it can see our entire path. It continuously guides us with instructions: take a turn, pause here, rest now, make a U-turn, go left, go right. It guides us during meditation and communicates through dreams, omens, synchronicities, angel numbers, and other signs. However, to receive these messages, we must stay connected to our Higher Self.

Our goal is to self-realize our power and our true nature and become like our Higher Self.

Many people ask me how they can connect with their Higher Self. The following is a meditation practice through which you can contact your Higher Self and seek guidance or information. You can repeat this practice whenever you feel confused, need clarity, or seek support from Higher Consciousness.

When there's no one around to help, listen, or when you feel incapable of sharing your situation with others, this exercise can help you connect with the Divine guidance that resides within each of us. It's freely available to everyone and doesn't require any external resources.

> ### Exercise 3.1 Guided Meditation: Connecting with Your Higher Self
>
> Begin by finding a quiet, comfortable space. Sit or lie down in a relaxed position. Close your eyes gently.
>
> 1. **Grounding and Breath Awareness**
>   a. Take a deep breath in... and slowly exhale.
>   b. Again, inhale deeply... and exhale gently.
>   c. With each breath, allow your body to relax and your mind to settle.
>   d. Feel your brain waves slowing down, your thoughts softening.
>   e. If any thoughts come to your awareness, gently refuse to dwell on them.
>   f. Let yourself arrive fully in this moment.

2. **Entering Presence**

    a. Now, bring your attention inward.

    b. Let go of the outside world.

    c. If any thoughts come to your awareness, gently refuse to dwell on them.

    d. Imagine yourself as pure Consciousness, free from roles, beliefs, labels, or limitations.

    e. You are simply being.

3. **Raising Your Vibration**

    a. To connect with higher frequencies, you must first elevate your own.

    b. Think of something you are deeply grateful for.

    c. It could be your parents, your pet, a loving relationship, your home, your education, your career, your car, your lifestyle, your health, or even the food you eat.

    d. Feel that gratitude in your heart.

    e. Let it expand and fill your entire being.

    f. Allow your brain and heart to align in this wave of emotion.

4. **Opening Your Energy Field**

    a. Now, open your energy field.

    b. Surrender all doubts, fears, and limiting beliefs.

    c. Release any reasoning or mental chatter about how or why.

Cheat Code to Manifest Miracles

d. Imagine you are holding a remote control of your Consciousness.

e. With intention, change the channel and shift into a state where you are pure Consciousness, limitless, just a field of energy, and deeply connected.

5. **Connecting with Your Higher Self**

   a. In this elevated state, you are now attuned to your Higher Self.

   b. Ask a question, make a request, or simply say: "What do I need to know right now that I don't yet see?"

   c. Then, listen.

   d. Be open.

   e. Watch what thoughts, feelings, or images arise.

   f. Your Higher Self speaks in subtle ways through intuition, symbols, and inner knowing.

6. **Closing the Practice**

   a. Take a few more deep breaths.

   b. Feel the energy you've connected with.

   c. Thank your Higher Self for its presence and guidance.

   d. When you're ready, gently bring your awareness back to the room.

   e. Open your eyes slowly, carrying this sense of connection with you.

If you are unsure about your Higher Self's response, try repeating this exercise the next night and ask for clearer signs, thoughts, or images.

Consciousness or Chetna

Consciousness, in simple terms, means awareness, and it is the only real thing in this Simulation. It is what is attached to this physical body that wants to experience everything. It is the awareness that lives in our body. Without it, our body will just wobble around. It perceives and experiences life and believes in this reality. It is attached to the physical body; therefore, it becomes ego-driven and thinks that we are all separated, that we are all different.

The soul never comes to the body (avatar); it's the Consciousness that stays in the body till we are alive. Our Consciousness has a frequency, and it continuously vibrates. It needs expansion if you want to manifest anything positive in life. Therefore, our Consciousness is the key to manifesting our desires in this physical reality. We will focus on Consciousness in this book.

Everything is vibrating, even solid objects like a rock, your table, chair, laptop, and car. Every atom in the Universe vibrates at a certain frequency. It's impossible for anything to stop vibrating and to reach zero frequency, unless we create an artificial scenario in a lab. Even the atoms in a dead body continue to vibrate, gradually transforming into something else. That's why nothing truly dies; it simply transforms.

Your Consciousness and its frequency of vibration are everything. Two people or beings that vibrate at the same frequency attract each other and can only sustain together if their frequencies match. The only difference between you and your desired reality is the difference in your frequencies. Everything exists in the present moment, but to see or receive it, you need to match and maintain that frequency to sustain it.

The Universe says yes to all your desires; it is not biased toward your desires. It is like a giant mirror that reflects the frequency of your Consciousness. If your Consciousness vibrates in a low or negative frequency, the Universe will also mirror it and will bring all negative and low-frequency things/people/situations into your reality. If you maintain your frequency high and stay positive even when the situation around you is negative or tough, eventually the Universe will start reflecting it with positive people/situations/things. After all, it's a Simulation, remember? It has certain rules, and all the avatars need to follow them to exist in this game of life.

The rules of this Divine Matrix apply equally to everyone. The Universe does not discriminate—whether you are rich or poor, the laws remain constant and impartial. Just as the Law of Gravity affects all beings without exception, so do the other universal laws. Gravity, for instance, is a fundamental rule within this Simulation. However, it does not operate in the same way outside of this simulated reality. What we perceive as natural laws here are simply the programmed mechanics of this Matrix.

Even in your difficult times, always remember that your Consciousness dictates the Universe; the Universe doesn't dictate your Consciousness—it only mirrors it. Therefore, always be mindful of what you are thinking, feeling, speaking, and imagining in your mind.

A bad event in the morning can trigger a chain of negative and bad experiences throughout the day, unless you make a conscious decision to break that chain and intentionally shift your mood and vibrations. The Universe does not lead—it follows. It mirrors your inner world with precision.

In truth, your Consciousness is the master key in this Matrix. If you want to feel the consciousness within you, practice stillness.

> **66**
>
> *You can feel the Divine Consciousness within when you're Still, Aware, Non-reactive, and Fully present in the Now.*
>
> **99**

You can feel the
Divine Consciousness
within when you're
Still, Aware,
Non-reactive, and
Fully Present
in the Now.

How to Prepare Yourself for Manifestation

 Forgive Yourself

 Use the Invisible Power of Words

 Break Free from the Mindset of Greed, Jealousy, Competition

 Set Intention

 Know What You Truly Want

 Prepare Your Avatar for Manifestation

CHAPTER 4

Prepare Yourself for Manifestation

Before you start manifesting miracles in your life, I want you to prepare yourself for that journey. If you don't plan and prepare yourself, you will not be able to manifest your desires. Don't skip this chapter, as it is crucial to get ready for a project before diving into its execution. As we all know, the success of any project relies heavily on its planning.

Forgive Yourself

Before you continue reading this book, it's important to understand that you cannot manifest anything positive while you are dealing with trauma or holding onto regrets from your past. You need to overcome trauma, anger, frustration, fear, and any negative thoughts that may be clouding your mind and judgment. The first step is to forgive yourself and others completely. Without forgiveness and the ability to let go of past regrets, true healing cannot happen. And without proper healing, manifestation is not possible.

Love yourself unconditionally, and where there is unconditional love, there is no judgment and no regrets. Accept your authenticity, and stop seeking approval and validation from others. You are complete and perfect, and you don't need anyone's approval to feel worthy or complete.

> *Exercise 4.1: Practice this exercise every evening until you fully accept and forgive yourself:*
>
> *Stand before the mirror, look deeply into your own eyes, and say the following with conviction:*
> *— I love and accept myself exactly as I am.*
> *— I forgive myself completely and unconditionally.*
> *— I choose to stand by myself, always—with compassion, courage, and grace.*

The Invisible Power of Words Shapes Our Reality

Understand the power of the words that you speak about yourself, your health, career, relationships, friendships, status, and finances every day. These are not just words; these are your beliefs about yourself and your future, and you are casting a spell every day about it. If the idea of casting spells doesn't resonate with you, consider these words as mantras that you repeat each day about yourself and your future.

Have you ever noticed that when you search for something online, you suddenly start seeing ads for it everywhere? That's Google's smart ad system that observes and responds to your searches and shows you related content. But something even more powerful happens in real life. When you keep thinking about something, like buying a blue car, you start seeing blue cars everywhere. Or you think of a song, and suddenly you hear it on the radio, or someone nearby starts singing it. Or you think about a topic, and your friend brings it up in conversation.

It's not a coincidence. It's the Universe responding to your observations, focus and energy.

Just like Google, the Universe has its own "search engine." It listens to your thoughts, feelings, and energy, and brings matching experiences into your life. What you observe and focus on, you begin to attract. Your attention is a powerful signal—and the Universe is always listening.

And it doesn't stop there. Your body is also listening, every moment of every day. The words you speak and the thoughts you think about yourself are heard first by you. Your body starts to match the energy and frequency of those words immediately. Even if no one else hears you, your body does. The Universe hears you. And they both start responding. So, be mindful. Be kind. Be intentional.

Be wise about the words you speak about yourself. These words shape your reality.

Your words are not just sounds; they are mantras and seeds that can invoke your soul. Your body, your life, and the Universe are always listening. What you say will be heard and responded to by your body immediately.

Never speak or think negatively about yourself. Anything that you say about yourself, starting with "I am," with feelings and emotions, manifests very quickly and easily because it shows your beliefs about yourself. If you say, "I want ..." it shows a sense of lacking, thus suggesting to the Universe that you don't have it, and this is something you simply desire or wish to have in the future. Therefore, always focus on positive affirmations about yourself. Say things like "I am getting better," "I am healing," "I am healthy," "I am wise," "I am wealthy," "I am love," "I am lovable," "I am famous," "I am beautiful," "I am worthy of all the love in the world," and "I am worthy of all the fame and success in the world."

That's why vision boards often don't work for many people. Instead of aligning them with the frequency of their desires, the boards simply serve as a reminder of what they want and what they don't have yet. Each time they look at it, it reinforces a sense of lacking—"I want this," or "I want this someday in the future," or "I don't have this yet"—rather than evoking the feeling of already living that reality. Without the emotional resonance of already

    Cheat Code to Manifest Miracles

having it, the vision remains a distant dream, not a magnet for manifestation.

When using vision boards, avoid viewing them from a place of lack or longing, as if your dreams are distant or yet to come. Instead, see them as a reflection of the version of you who already lives that reality. Let them serve as a reminder to align your energy, thoughts, and emotions with the frequency of someone who has already manifested those visions in the present moment.

Avoid saying things like "I am dumb," "I am stupid," "I am unlucky," "I am jinxed," "I am a loser," "I am weird," "I am crazy," "I will never succeed," "I will never get better," "I am dying," "I wish I could do that," "I can never do that," "I never get good seats," etc. Your thoughts create a frequency as soon as they come out of your physical mind and start attracting things and experiences into your life. You can measure this frequency with the help of an EEG test. The easiest and quickest person to attract with these thoughts is yourself, so anything you say about yourself can begin to manifest almost immediately.

When you say, "I'm unlucky," the Universe listens and begins to bring more situations that make you feel unlucky. When you say, "I'm not well," your body hears it and starts to respond by falling sick. When you say, "I'll never succeed," the Universe starts creating experiences that lead to failure. Your words are impactful. They carry energy. Be mindful of every word that leaves your mouth. Because even when no one else is listening, you are. Your body is listening. And the Universe is always listening. Everything you say about yourself should be positive and expressed in the present tense, as if you already possess it or are experiencing it now. By consistently repeating these affirmations, especially before going to bed or right after waking up, you will begin to reprogram your subconscious mind and reshape your belief system. This simple yet powerful practice can significantly improve your mindset and transform your life.

Change the habit of speaking negatively about yourself and others immediately. When we talk about our problems, we make them even bigger. Whenever you catch yourself gossiping or saying something unkind, pause and correct yourself. Rephrase your negative words into positive ones. Speak with kindness, speak with awareness. Remember, we are all connected. There is no real separation between us, only the illusion of individuality. We are all part of one Consciousness, one Energy, one Source. So, when you speak ill of someone, you're not just affecting them; you're affecting yourself.

Every word you say about others sends energy back to you. When you gossip, judge, or send negative vibrations, you're actually hurting yourself.

There's a beautiful ancient Mayan saying that captures this truth perfectly:

In lak'ech, Ala k'in

This means, "I am you, as you are me," or "I am another you, as you are another me."

In Matthew 22:39 (KJV), Jesus says:

"Thou shalt love thy neighbour as thyself."

This means: *"You shall love your neighbour as yourself."* At its core, this teaching reveals a profound truth — you are your neighbour. There is no separation between you and others; Jesus is referring to everyone else when He says "the neighbour." We are all expressions of the same Divine Consciousness, interconnected and unified. To love another is to love yourself. To harm another is to harm yourself.

Treat others with the same care, respect, and consideration you would want for yourself — because in truth, they are you.

Exercise 4.2: Your Sankalp Challenge

— *Write down nine (9) positive affirmations about yourself that you want to manifest.*

— *Commit to speaking them aloud six (6) times a day for the next twenty (21) days without fail. This is your Sankalp, your sacred commitment.*

> *— It is a scientifically proven fact that repeating something consistently for twenty (21) days can lead to changes in your DNA. You have the power to rewrite your DNA and transform yourself.*
>
> *— Just as negative habits, thoughts, and words can alter your DNA, positive habits, thoughts, and affirmations about yourself can also create profound change.*
>
> *— Your DNA is like a storage system for your Consciousness, holding Sanskaras—memories from every lifetime, including ancestral trauma.*
>
> *— By consciously choosing your affirmations, you begin to reprogram this sacred system and awaken your highest potential.*

Break Free from the Mindset of Greed, Jealousy, and Competition

Adopt a mindset of collaboration instead of competition. When you see someone succeeding in their manifestations or achieving their dreams, do not get jealous or envious of their success; let it inspire you. Collaborate with them and learn from their experiences. Remember, if they can do it, you can too. The sun shines on everyone equally, and everyone receives the blessings of the Universe in the same measure.

You cannot change the Universe or ask God to withhold blessings from others; the only person you can change

   Cheat Code to Manifest Miracles

is yourself. Abundance is unlimited, opportunities are limitless, but you need to be aware and alert to recognize them. Do not look for an easy way or shortcuts. Do not become settled in your comfort zone if you desire to achieve something big.

Do not compromise your moral values or integrity. Don't emulate others or compare yourself to them. Maintain your authenticity.

How many times have you noticed that a simple-looking actor, anchor, podcast host, singer, or a leader looks so charismatic and attracts everyone with just their authenticity, personality, their communication skills, their expressions and emotions, or their wit?

Do you think these successful people try to imitate someone else or try to look like someone else?

No.

Because they are authentic and even in plain, normal, single-colored clothes, they shine and attract masses like a magnet.

Never be a wannabe. Be authentic!

Set Intention

Setting intentions is one of the most important steps in your manifestation journey. If you want to experience miracles every day, begin each morning by setting a clear intention. After you wake up, take a moment to tell the Universe how you want your day to unfold.

Before starting any activity, pause and ask yourself:

Why am I doing this? What do I want to receive from it?

Whether it's a job interview, a meeting, or an audition—set your intention. What outcome are you hoping for? Even during simple moments, like boarding a flight, take a few seconds before takeoff to set your intention.

You might say to yourself:

"I want this journey to be safe and smooth," or "I am going to reach my destination safely and on time."

Take two minutes to go deep within yourself. If necessary, close your eyes and focus on setting your intention before you begin any activity. When your intentions are clear, the Universe understands exactly what you want. And only then can it begin to help you manifest it.

You need to have a clear intention or a strong desire for something in order to manifest it. Without a burning desire, it will be difficult to focus, maintain discipline, or take action during the manifestation process. When someone has a burning desire and firmly believes that they can see themselves living that reality, miracles happen.

When you don't have a burning desire to achieve something, or you have too many desires that you are focusing on at once, you will struggle to concentrate on any single goal and may not take it seriously. As a result, you will quickly lose the energy needed to manifest it and may become distracted by other goals, desires, or situations.

Furthermore, having a burning desire for something is a sign that what you want already exists in your future. Right now, you're just at the starting point of bringing it into your present life. Even if you've only just begun thinking about it, it's already waiting for you in another timeline. So, think of it like reverse engineering; what you desire has already happened in your future, and now you're simply taking steps to reach it.

Remember, time does not move in a straight line. The past, present, and future all exist simultaneously. So, always imagine that your desire is already manifested in another timeline. In this moment, you are simply beginning your journey toward it. This perspective will provide you with complete certainty that what you are trying to manifest has already come to fruition in your future, and you are worthy of achieving it.

Know What You Truly Want

You need to have a clear picture of what you want to manifest. Whatever you can imagine and manifest in your mind through visualization, you can manifest it easily in your physical reality. This is a law of the Universe. Most of the time, we only think and imagine negative thoughts or fears, worrying about something that might go wrong. Consciously replace every negative thought with a positive one.

For example, if you want to manifest a house, start by writing down all the details clearly. Think about

- what kind of house do you want
- the location or neighborhood
- how many bedrooms do you need
- what your bedroom will look like
- how your children's room will be
- where your parents or guests will stay
- whether you need a small office at home
- the interior design or theme for each room
- the colors of the curtains and wallpapers
- the view from your balcony
- how your kitchen and living room will look.

Try to imagine everything in great detail. The clearer your vision, the stronger your manifestation.

Exercise 4.3: Define Your Vision Statement

— *Begin by clearly writing down in detail what you want to manifest. Focus on the outcome of your desire and describe it thoroughly.*

— *Once written, read it aloud several times, then review it mentally multiple times.*

— *If anything feels off or doesn't resonate, revise your statement until it feels aligned with your inner truth.*

> *— Next, visualize your desire while fully experiencing the emotions and feelings associated with it. Ask yourself: Is this truly what I want to manifest in my life?*
>
> *— If the answer is no, modify your vision statement and repeat the process.*
>
> *— If the answer is yes, this becomes your vision statement—the miracle you wish to manifest in your future.*

This exercise will help you gain clarity about your purpose and give you a crystal-clear goal to manifest. Having this kind of clarity is a key step toward living a successful and fulfilling life.

Prepare Your Avatar for Manifestation

Your avatar, representing you in the game of life, consists of both a body and a Consciousness. Some spiritual teachings refer to this avatar as a "vessel." Your Consciousness resides within your vessel, so it is important to prepare and support it to manifest your intentions effectively.

To achieve this, live a healthy lifestyle and focus on consuming natural foods that are easy for your body to digest. This allows your body to concentrate on visualization and taking action, rather than spending excessive time sleeping and digesting food. Engage in regular exercise, and avoid unhealthy foods, toxic friendships, harmful habits, and limiting societal norms, beliefs, and mainstream news.

By maintaining a healthy lifestyle, meditating, focusing on your goals, and surrounding yourself with inspiring people who have achieved success in various fields, you empower yourself. This motivation raises your energy and frequency, preparing you to lead a miraculous life every day.

Remember, your body is a machine provided for you to play this game of life. If you abuse or neglect it, it will wear out or break down, preventing you from fully participating in the experience.

☑ *Daily Healthy Habits Checklist*

- *Set your intention for the day*
- *Drink water first thing in the morning*
- *Eat fresh, natural foods*
- *Move your body (walk, stretch, or exercise)*
- *Do something creative each day*
- *Meditate or sit in silence for 15 minutes. Let go of everything—labels, responsibilities, and problems—during this time.*
- *Pause before reacting to any negative situation*
- *Avoid negative content and toxic influences*
- *Take one inspired action toward your goal*
- *Reflect and express gratitude before bed*

CHAPTER 5

Prayers Are Not What You Think

Prayer is a way to communicate with the Creator or the Universe. When you want to ask something or discuss something in your prayers, always ask without any hidden agenda. Be open and crystal clear about what it is that you want. There is a way to ask and communicate with the Universe.

The Universe only understands the language of your feelings, emotions, and frequency. That's the language of the Universe. Therefore, do not pray with negative emotions, such as crying, weeping, yelling, or sobbing, as this will only attract low-frequency energies and things and bring more situations that prompt you to cry, weep, yell, and sob.

It's natural to feel broken and shattered at times and ask for help from God with tears in our eyes; however, try not to make this a habit, as such emotions signify fear. Most of the time, it's our mind that is generating these fears simply by negative thinking and negative emotions about the future.

Your prayers should look like this: Communicate directly and openly with the Universe, without hidden motives. Imagine the outcome you wish to manifest with vivid feelings and emotions—as if it has already happened and you are living that reality in the present moment. Your visualization should reflect peace, certainty, and alignment—not stress or anxious waiting. You are not hoping for something to happen; instead, you are embodying the truth that it already has. Speak and visualize with confidence, knowing you are worthy of receiving the blessings.

> **_Worry is a form of manifestation—what you fear, you attract_**

Most of us live in fear: fear of failing, being rejected, left alone, separated, or not being good enough. But you don't have to live like that. These fears are part of the lessons your soul chose before coming into this life. They're here to help you grow. Live fearlessly with courage, knowing that whatever is meant for you, whether it's love, success, healing, or wealth, will come to you at the right time. And what's not meant for you will leave, no matter how hard you try to hold on.

Cheat Code to Manifest Miracles

Whatever blessing is meant for you—be it your soulmate, dream career, radiant health, or anything else—will always find its way to you. No one can take it away. It might be somewhere else or with someone else right now, but once you align your energy with what you truly desire, it will come to you. What's yours is already on its way.

Make it a habit to gently pull yourself away from negative thoughts and fear. Focus on what brings you joy. Be thankful for what you already have. Shift your energy to positive thoughts and ask the Universe to bring you the miracles and blessings you deserve.

Whenever you find yourself feeling confused or uncertain, remember—you are never alone. Support and guidance are always available to you. Just as we have tools like AI assistants (e.g., ChatGPT, Gemini) at our fingertips, we also have access to our Higher Self and Guardian Angels at all times. They are always present, patiently waiting for your permission to assist. Invite them in. Ask for their help. You are divinely supported. To establish this connection, refer to Exercises 3.1 and 5.2.

Remember, your consciousness and perceptions shape your reality. You co-create with the Universe through your thoughts and observations. The Universe does not dictate your consciousness—it is your consciousness that dictates the Universe. So, always feel confident and worthy of your desires. Feel worthy that you deserve your blessings and demand them from the Universe when you pray. Just be crystal clear about what you want to manifest and communicate the same in your prayers.

Do not ask or pray for others to change; always seek to change yourself. When you change, your thoughts, emotions, and feelings will also change—which will raise your frequency and reshape your belief system. Ultimately, this will lead to a change in your reality. You must be the change you wish to see in the world, as the world is merely a reflection of your perception.

Jalāl al-Dīn Muḥammad Rūmī, commonly known as Rumi, was a 13th-century Persian poet, Islamic scholar, and Sufi mystic. Rumi once said,

---

***Everything in the universe is within you,
ask from yourself.***

Everything you desire in life is already within you. So why cry, beg, plead, or worry when you pray? The Universe and the Divine already reside within you. Pray with confidence—because you are the source and you are asking yourself. All you need to do is focus on self-improvement. With the right mindset and positive thoughts embedded in your subconscious, you can attract the right opportunities and experiences from the Universe. Your subconscious mind functions like a magnet; it attracts anything and everything that vibrates in the same frequency as yours from your surroundings.

Instead of focusing on others or trying to change people, situations, or control outcomes, your highest priority should be to work on yourself. As you elevate your inner world, your outer reality will naturally begin to transform.

The best way to pray is to tell the Universe or God what you want, by imagining it with feelings and emotions through your visualization. Make sure when you are visualizing, you are imagining in the present moment, "NOW." Like it's already done. Imagine it with complete confidence, like a child who has no fear or shame while asking. God is within you, so you are asking from yourself. There is no need to beg or feel guilty when you are asking from yourself.

Then, surrender and let go. Never become fixated on the outcome or how it should happen. The outcome or the result is never in your hands. The Universe works in mysterious ways; let it decide what is good for you and your life's journey.

> ***The more you try to control the out come
> or someone else's reality,
> the more it slips out of your hands.
> That's the law of this Simulation we call life.***

When you release attachment to the outcome, you open yourself to receiving more, and often better than what you originally asked for. Always remember, the Universe is working for you and through you. It is never against you. Don't try to swim against the current; instead, allow the Universe to work its magic through you. That way, it will find the shortest and easiest path to bring your miracles to life.

<table>
<tr><td>

Exercise 5.1: Nighttime Visualization Practice

— *Before going to bed, visualize what you want or communicate with God or the Universe.*

— *Always frame your question positively and imagine it with clarity and intention. Avoid asking or visualizing from a place of negativity, scarcity, or fear. Never imagine a negative situation in your visualization.*

— *After your visualization, surrender the question and ask the Universe to provide an answer. The response may come in various forms—through dreams, a phone call, a conversation with a friend, a sign or billboard, angel numbers, or omens.*

— *If you don't receive an answer, ask again the following night. Let the Universe know you didn't understand the previous message and request a clearer signal.*

</td></tr>
</table>

    Cheat Code to Manifest Miracles

— If you're asking a yes-or-no type of question, ask the Universe to send you a specific signal for yes. Repeat this for three (3) nights and then wait.

— If you still don't get your answer, try repeating the process after a week.

A Miracle Named Pluto

I want to share a deeply personal chapter of my life with you. For almost a year, I struggled with depression, anxiety, and persistent panic attacks. My body echoed my emotional turmoil, persistent migraines, and neck and shoulder pain that grew so severe that I struggled to maintain my body's balance. I sought help from renowned neurosurgeons and psychiatrists, desperate for relief. But nothing seemed to work.

In search of comfort, I moved from Bangalore to Mumbai, hoping that being closer to family would ease the pain. But even after settling in Mumbai, the migraines and depression persisted. I felt lost, confused, and exhausted in my own body and mind. One day, in a moment of surrender, I closed my eyes and asked the Universe for help. I didn't know what I needed. Just a sign, a vision, or something to guide me out of the darkness. After that meditation, a quiet thought began to surface repeatedly: Bring a dog into your life. It felt like a whisper from the Universe, a gentle nudge toward healing. I knew in my heart this was the miracle I had asked for.

I searched everywhere, newspapers, websites, adoption listings, and soon found someone offering puppies for adoption. Without hesitation, I brought one home. My family named him Pluto, inspired by my love for planets, stars, and Astrology. And then, something extraordinary happened.

For an entire week, I forgot to take my medications, the ones I couldn't miss even for a day without triggering nightmares, migraines, and panic attacks. Yet, that week passed peacefully. No pain. No fear. No darkness. It was only later that I realized I had stopped taking my meds. Pluto had brought light into my life with him—the healing I had been searching for. The Universe had answered me not with words, but with a wagging tail and unconditional love.

Pluto isn't just a pet. He is my miracle. He reminded me that miracles and healing don't always come in the forms we expect; they can arrive quietly, wrapped in fur, with eyes full of love. Every time I look at Pluto, I'm reminded that the Universe is always listening. All we have to do is ask.

How to Ask from Your Higher Self and Guardian Angels

You can also seek help from your Higher Self and angels if you're feeling confused in life or struggling to find answers to your problems. When you don't know what to do or which path to choose, remember, as mentioned in the previous chapters, we all have a Higher Self guiding us throughout our life's journey. Follow the meditation mentioned in Chapter 3 to connect with your Higher Self.

In addition to the Higher Self, every individual has Guardian Angels assigned to each one of us to guide and assist them in completing our life's journey. These Guardian Angels could be your ancestors or members of your soul family. Everyone has access to their guides and angels. Consider them as customer care service agents who are waiting for your call and will answer your prayer when you make the call and seek help. But remember, you have to call them in order to establish the connection. For example, if your cable TV connection breaks down, you will have to call the cable company and ask them to fix it. Similarly, angels and guides cannot help unless you call and grant them permission. They watch over you and observe, but you must explicitly permit them and ask for their assistance before they can intervene in your destiny.

To ask for help and guidance from your Guardian Angels, do the following:

Exercise 5.2: Calling Your Guardian Angels

— *Sit comfortably, take a few deep breaths, and quieten your mind. Focus inward, directing your energy to your heart.*

— *Now, imagine dialing a number and making a call to your Guardian Angels. Feel the calm as the connection is made.*

— Choose any angel number that resonates with you—such as 333, 1111, 222, 888, 121, 1221, or my personal favorite, 311—to initiate the call.

— Begin speaking to them. Share your situation openly, without any hidden agenda, and then give them clear permission to intervene in your life.

— Ask for guidance or a sign or evidence or anything simple that comes to mind.

This practice has helped me many times. For instance, I once asked my angels to give me a sign by showing me a keychain within an hour if I was meant to move forward with a decision. Just a few minutes later, I met a friend who was holding a keychain in a very noticeable way. It was engraved with the sacred symbol OM. It was the sign I needed. I felt calm, deeply reassured, and hopeful that I had made the right choice.

> **"**
> *Trust that the Universe and your Guardian Angels
> are always watching over you and listening.
> All you need to do is use your childlike
> imagination, ask sincerely,
> and give them permission to intervene
> in your destiny and help you.*
> **"**

Prayers expand your Consciousness and enhance the vessel that God has given you in this life. As your Consciousness expands and evolves, it can hold more Divine light and grace, allowing miracles to unfold and your desires to manifest in your life naturally. Prayer provides you with the strength to improve yourself and the courage to overcome any challenges you may face. Without an expanded Consciousness, creating miracles is not possible. Therefore, praying in the right way is a crucial step in manifesting miracles and should not be overlooked.

CHAPTER 6

Manifestation Code

The Power of Intention: My Journey to a Dream Home in Mumbai

I've always been interested in real estate since I started working. The idea of owning a luxurious apartment was a dream I held close to my heart.

When I was just 24 years old, I manifested a big and beautiful penthouse in Bangalore, reflecting the abundance I was attracting into my life. However, as my career took me on extensive travels across the U.S. and other countries, the space remained largely unused. Eventually, I decided to rent it out, but when I moved to Mumbai, managing the property from a distance became more of a liability than a joy.

That's when I realized that if I wanted to settle down in Mumbai, I should buy an apartment here where I am currently living. But with property prices constantly skyrocketing in Mumbai, it felt nearly impossible to turn the desire of owning an apartment in Mumbai into reality. I needed to sell the penthouse and let go of what no longer aligned with my journey and start manifesting a new goal.

For ten years, I tried to sell the penthouse. But being located slightly on the outskirts and having a large area due to its penthouse layout, it didn't attract buyers easily. I wasn't actively pushing for the sale either—I was in a laid-back mode, trusting that when the time was right, it would be sold. Meanwhile, I continued renting an apartment in Mumbai, holding onto the vision of owning a space that truly felt like home. Deep down, I knew the Universe was aligning things in its own time.

One day, my landlord suddenly raised the rent and gave me an ultimatum: either pay the new amount or leave. I initially felt frustrated by his attitude, but instead of reacting or slipping into victimhood, I chose to stay calm. I saw it as a sign—maybe it was time to seriously consider buying my own home in Mumbai. At that moment, I set a clear intention and asked the Universe for guidance. I had always wanted to buy a home in Mumbai, but until then, it had remained a vague wish. This time, I did things differently. I turned that wish into a focused, burning desire.

I began by setting a clear intention and consciously visualizing my dream home in Mumbai. I meditated on this desire for hours that day, imagining it as if it were already mine. I told myself with complete certainty and a calm mind:

'This is happening now. I can't wait any longer for it to happen someday in the future. I am ready to take whatever action it requires me to take.'

That moment marked a shift—from passive hoping to active manifesting.

To my surprise, the very next day, I received a phone call from someone living on the ground floor of the same building where my penthouse was located. He was looking to upgrade and was genuinely interested in buying my penthouse—the very property I hadn't been able to sell for ten years!

He had already checked the property, studied the market, and was ready to move forward immediately. It felt surreal, as if the Universe had been waiting for me to set a clear intention before aligning everything perfectly. Within fifteen days, everything was finalized. Before my two-month notice period with the landlord ended, I had sold my old property in Bangalore and bought a beautiful new apartment in Mumbai. It was in a prime location with views of mountains, waterfalls, and a garden—something almost impossible to find in a city like Mumbai.

This experience taught me the true power of conscious thinking, staying calm, setting intentions, focused energy, and taking action instead of procrastinating. When you stop doubting and start believing in your intentions, the Universe begins to move things in your favor.

Now that you understand how reality works, and you're prepared to manifest miracles, let's explore a simple Manifestation code in this chapter. This code gives you a clear understanding of how manifestation works within our Simulation or the Divine Matrix.

As I mentioned earlier, Consciousness is key to manifestation. When we combine this Consciousness with the power of our subconscious mind, we produce certain frequencies that go out into the Universe. These frequencies begin to attract people, situations, and things into our lives that match them, initiating the manifestation process. All these people, situations, and objects already exist; they simply become visible to us when we vibrate at certain frequencies.

> *Consciousness simply means awareness with a choice. When you take control of your mind and thoughts, you create the framework upon which manifestation occurs. It's not just about wishing—it's about consciously directing your energy, aligning your inner world, and choosing your thoughts with intention. That's when manifestation becomes a natural outcome of your awakened state*

Manifestation doesn't mean creating something that doesn't already exist or bringing something from other dimensions. Your soulmate already exists. Your dream car already exists. Your dream home already exists. Your dream job already exists. The body in which you want to manifest perfect health already exists. Everything exists here and now. Instead, it simply means we remove the frequencies that previously blocked our manifestations by choosing to vibrate at a different frequency. This shift allows us to stop attracting what we don't want and start attracting the situations we desire.

What you seek, is seeking you.

This quote from Rumi is perfect in terms of manifestation. Everything in the external world is an illusion. Everything you desire to see or experience: your reality, including universal and scientific laws, is part of this grand illusion. What you seek, you will find. Everything exists now, in the present moment. All that you want already exists and is also seeking you in this very moment. Everything you desire to experience is already present, existing in various states—either visible or invisible. What determines its visibility is the frequency of the vibration you are embodying.

On a material level, consider this: If you want to buy a Lamborghini, remember that the car manufacturer is also seeking potential buyers who can buy their cars. If you want to buy a luxurious home, remember that the builder of your dream property is also looking for a buyer like you. Similarly, if you aspire to be famous, fame is also searching for someone who is worthy of that spotlight, or if you are trying to find a new perfect job, that employer is also looking for a suitable candidate. The same goes for love; if you are in search of a soulmate, know that your soulmate is also seeking the same unconditional love.

So ultimately, it comes down to the frequency at which you are vibrating that brings things, situations, and people to you. Now, let's see how to produce the frequencies we want to broadcast into the Universe. The answer is through visualization and the power of your subconscious mind. Your subconscious mind then behaves like a radio, transmitting and receiving the frequency of your conscious thoughts. It starts attracting people and opportunities that resonate with those frequencies. This is when the Universe starts presenting you with opportunities that will eventually lead you to your manifestations. However, it's important to recognize these opportunities and take action when they arise.

The Manifestation Code is as follows:

> *Manifestation = Visualization + Action*
>
> *Manifestation is a process that combines the power of visualization with intentional and inspired actions in the physical world.*

Now let's break down this code and understand each component in detail.

Visualization

It always starts with curiosity, and then the curiosity becomes a thought. When you concentrate and focus on that thought and keep thinking about it, it turns into a conscious thought. Now, when you mix this conscious thought with your energy, feelings, and emotions, and start imagining this thought in your mind, it is called visualization. Therefore,

> *Visualization = Awareness + Thoughts + Feelings + Imagination*

Always remember, you are constantly manifesting 24/7 through your thoughts. Our thoughts generate energy, and whatever we consistently and consciously think becomes part of our reality. Just as positive thoughts, emotions, and feelings attract positive outcomes into your reality, negative thoughts like fear, jealousy, scarcity, stress, and anxiety can lead to negative manifestations in your life. Therefore, if you keep visualizing negative things, ideas, or outcomes, even those will manifest in your life.

You need to be extremely aware and cautious of your thoughts, feelings, and emotions at all times. You must actively and consciously remove any negative beliefs, thoughts, or feelings that come into your mind with positive ones. When a negative thought or feeling comes to your mind, try to change it right away. Think about someone you love, remember a time when you did something great, helped someone, or imagine a happy future. Don't listen to sad songs or watch emotional movies; they can make you feel worse. Instead, play a happy song, or watch something fun and uplifting, or watch/listen to a motivational podcast. You can also do something creative, like cooking a healthy meal or doing simple house chores. These small actions can help you feel better, give you a sense of achievement, and gently bring your focus back to something positive and to the present moment.

Don't go into victim mode or seek approval from others. Avoid calling people to explain your situation or posting sad and negative videos. Instead, remind yourself that this is all part of a bigger plan. Your soul chose this journey before coming into this life. This is your reality, and everything that's happening is helping you grow and learn. But this reality isn't as real as it seems; it's more like a movie. In every movie, the hero feels low at some point, but things always change. Just like that, your story will change, too.

> *Thoughts are like pop-up windows on your mental screen. Don't double-click on the negative ones— they'll corrupt your system. Acknowledge them, then close them without engagement.*

Cheat Code to Manifest Miracles

The Role of the Subconscious Mind

Everything begins with a thought. Every discovery or invention that has ever happened was sparked by curiosity, and then it transformed into a thought or idea. When you keep visualizing a thought or idea, whether positive or negative, using your feelings and emotions, it goes into your subconscious mind. Repetition is key in transferring thoughts to your subconscious. Once in your subconscious, these thoughts generate frequencies that go outward into the Universe.

Your subconscious acts like a hunting dog, instinctively tracking people, situations, ideas, and objects that resonate with those frequencies.

You may have noticed a strange feeling when you're very tired or stressed and are just about to fall asleep. As your brain begins to enter a dream-like state, it can create sensations of movement, even though your body isn't actually moving. You might feel like you're falling, or imagine moving your hand, and suddenly, your body reacts by jerking your hand or leg to prevent you from falling. This occurs because your subconscious mind cannot distinguish between what is real and what is vividly imagined.

When you visualize something with strong emotions, your subconscious treats it as a real experience. It begins to influence your thoughts, feelings, and even your physical reactions. This is why visualization is such a powerful tool.

If you want to manifest a healthy, lean, strong, and fit body, it's essential to visualize yourself and your health in a positive way. Your body will begin to respond accordingly. Don't worry about how long it will take, or whether you can exercise or follow a diet. These thoughts only slow you down. Instead, write down your goal in a simple, clear sentence. Then, imagine often—through your mind's eye—that you are healthy, lean, strong, and fit. Let this vision become a natural part of your thinking. This helps your subconscious mind believe it's possible. When the right moment comes, take action and give it your best. You might choose to eat better, join a yoga class, or start working out. Your body will follow the path your mind has already created.

Exercise 6.1: Programming the Subconscious

— *Write down your intention in great detail so you know exactly what you want to manifest. This clarity will guide your visualization, making it crystal clear what you want to imagine.*

— *Once your intention is written, begin your visualization practice:*

— Write down your intention in great detail so you know exactly what you want to manifest. This clarity will guide your visualization, making it crystal clear what you want to imagine.

— Once your intention is written, begin your visualization practice:

  ❖ *Sit comfortably, take a few deep breaths, and calm your mind.*

  ❖ *Turn inward, directing your energy toward your heart.*

  ❖ *Visualize your intention as if it is already happening in the present moment.*

  ❖ *See yourself living it, experiencing it fully.*

  ❖ *Feel the joy, peace, and excitement—add your emotions and immerse yourself in the scene, as if it were a movie playing in a theater.*

— When you're done, express gratitude to the Universe, gently return from your meditation, and open your eyes.

— Repeating this process will help embed your intention into your subconscious mind, aligning your energy with the reality you wish to create.

Action

When the Universe starts doing its job of bringing and attracting opportunities, people, and situations in your life, you need to do your part in identifying those opportunities and taking action. You cannot expect an idea to manifest itself without you taking any action, and only by visualizing it in your mind. Taking action is equally important.

For example, if you want to open a restaurant, let's say the Universe brings you someone ready to invest in your restaurant idea. But after that, you must take action to open the restaurant, like finding an ideal place to open the restaurant, completing legal formalities, signing the agreement, closing the deal, recruiting chefs and waiters, finalizing the interiors and exteriors, finalizing the cuisines and menu, taking care of kitchen equipment, marketing your new business, etc. You must recognize opportunities and act on them while the door is still open, because once it closes, that door may close quickly and may not open again anytime soon.

Have you heard about the Red Car Theory? Many success coaches and motivational speakers use it to highlight the importance of noticing opportunities. The theory is based on a simple idea: When you start thinking about buying a red car, you suddenly begin to see red cars everywhere. (You can replace "red car" with any color you like—blue, yellow, etc.) This happens not because there are suddenly more red cars on the road, but because your mind is now focused on noticing them. This simple concept teaches us that opportunities are all around us, but we only recognize them when we actively look for them.

To understand the Red Car Theory, begin with a simple experiment. Ask yourself, "How many red cars did I notice today?" Like most people, you might answer, "I don't remember seeing any." However, the interesting part comes when you start actively looking for red cars. You'll soon realize they are everywhere, almost as if they've appeared out of nowhere. You may even begin to notice cars that aren't red, but are close, such as maroon, pink, and similar shades of red.

To manifest anything, remember that it all starts with a thought. When you consciously visualize that thought repeatedly, it enters your subconscious mind. As you start getting opportunities, you need to act on them.

Manifestation = Visualization + Action

Visualization is

 Awareness

 Thoughts

 Feelings

 Imagination

Mastering the Matrix Requires
Complete Certainty
Authenticity
Aligned Mindset
Unconditional Love

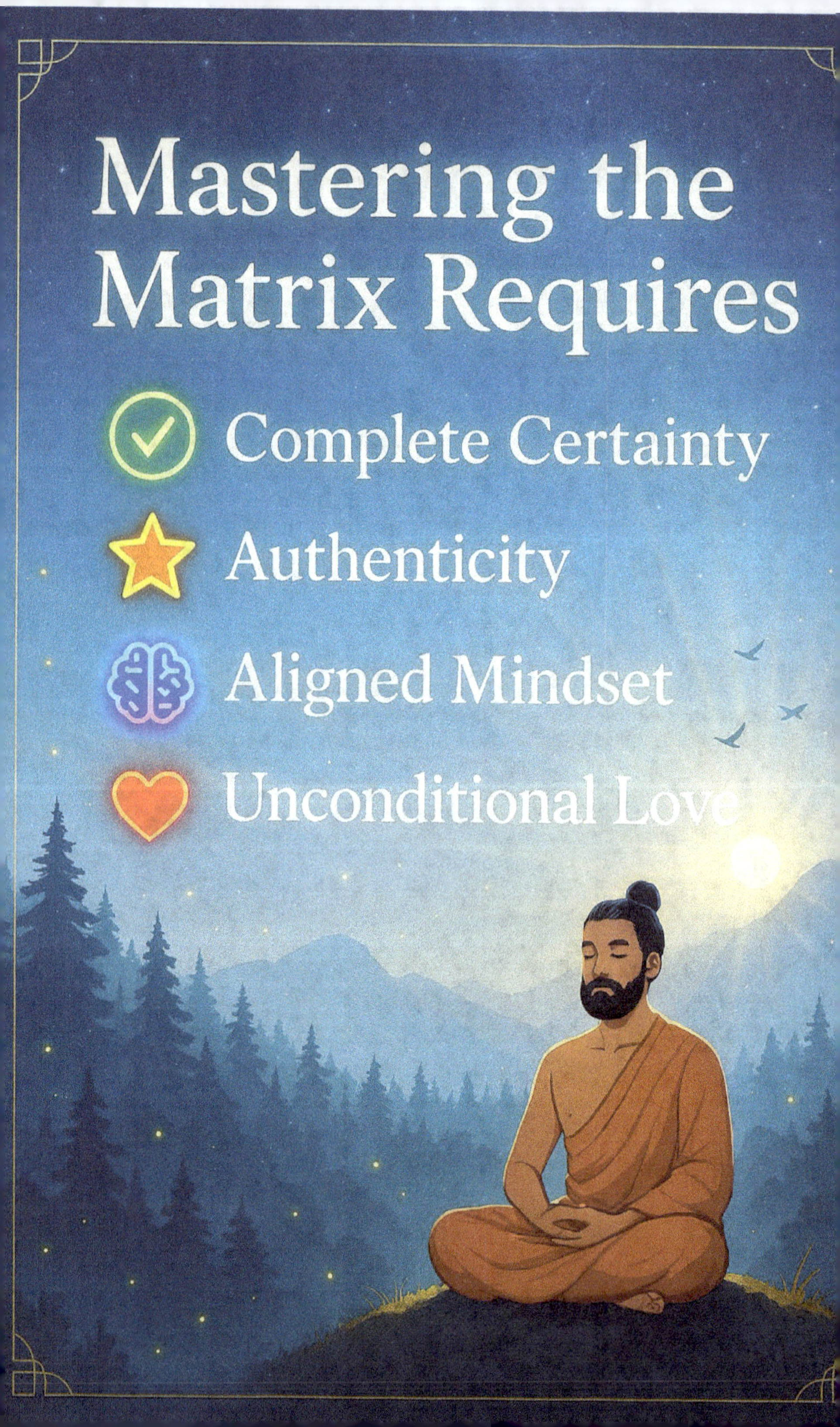

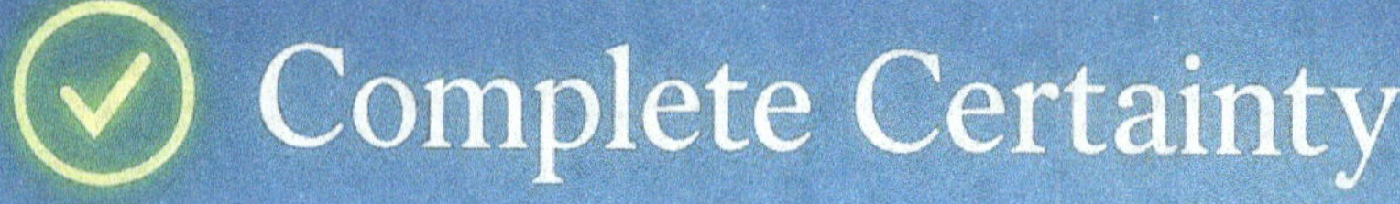

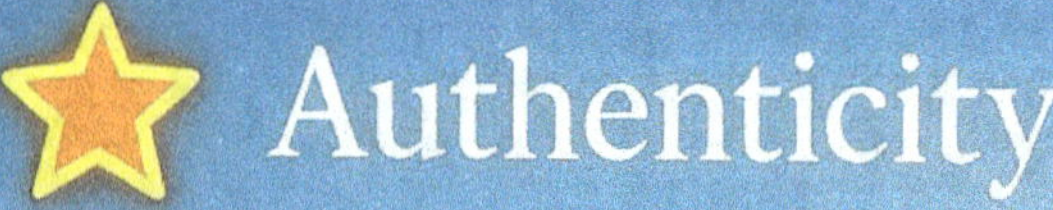

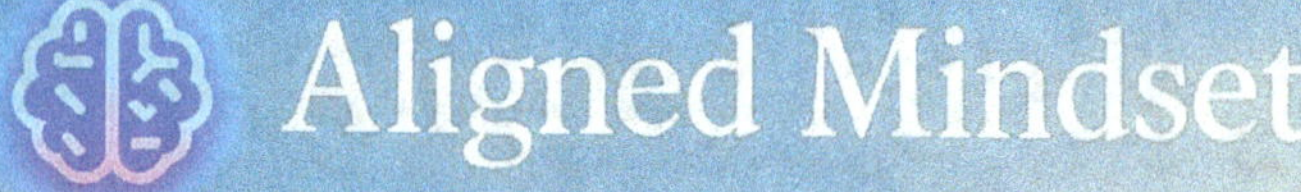

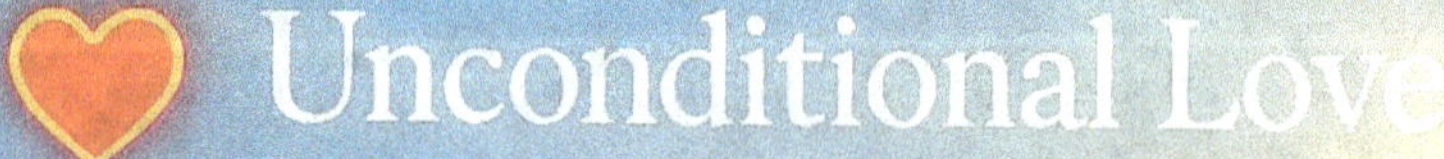

CHAPTER 7

Mastering the Matrix: The Art of Skipping Soul Tests and Creating Miracles

In this chapter, I'm going to share with you some secret ingredients that will support you throughout your manifestation journey. These are not just tools; they are soul codes, energetic keys that help you navigate the Divine Matrix with grace and clarity. Without these ingredients, it isn't possible to produce a true miracle. Furthermore, if, for some reason, something miraculous does occur in your life without these elements, you will likely be unable to sustain the outcome of that miracle over time.

Your journey may feel long, and at times, deeply painful. But if you truly want to master the Matrix and rise above the tests and challenges it throws at you daily, these ingredients are essential. They will help you shift your perception, stay calm in the storm, and unlock miracles without having to suffer through every lesson.

Complete Certainty

Remember, it was your soul that chose to enter this world. Before birth, your soul carefully selected specific experiences from the Divine catalogue—lessons, relationships, divorce, professional and health challenges, poverty, opportunities, and even a traumatic or abusive childhood. These were chosen not to punish you, but to help you grow, evolve, and become a co-creator of your reality.

This means your reality isn't random. It's a reflection of your soul's choices. Whether you experience joy or frustration, remain single or enter a relationship, face ease or struggle—it's all part of the path your soul chose to walk.

But here's the key: if you are the one making these choices at the soul level, then what part of you can help change or upgrade those choices in this lifetime?

It is your Consciousness.

As your Consciousness evolves and expands, and as you fill it with the light of creation and Divine grace, you begin to shift your reality. You awaken to your power. You stop reacting and start creating. You move from being a passive participant to an active co-creator with the Universe.

The next question that arises is:

How do we expand our Consciousness with light and Divine grace?

   Cheat Code to Manifest Miracles

We expand our Consciousness not through force, but through surrender—by letting go of resisting and remaining steady in faith and unwavering in hope, even when life doesn't unfold as we expect. The key is "Complete Certainty".

Certainty is a sacred spiritual tool. It opens the gates to Divine grace and elevates our frequency to receive higher wisdom. When we trust deeply—beyond logic, beyond appearances—we align with the truth that everything is happening in perfect harmony with our soul's agreement.

Whatever you're experiencing right now, know that you and your soul chose it for your growth. Every challenge, delay, or detour is a divine setup for expansion. When you embrace this truth, your Consciousness begins to rise, and grace flows effortlessly into your life. Hold "Complete Certainty" that you will manifest either exactly what you desire, something similar, or something even better. The Universe always responds to the vibration of your trust

Certainty is the one quality all great souls and legends have in common; they always knew they would succeed one day. It is what carried them through the darkest times. So, no matter how difficult your current situation may be, hold unwavering certainty that things will improve. Trust that your miracle will manifest at the perfect time, once your soul has received the lessons it came here to learn.

Certainty doesn't mean you'll receive exactly what you desire in the way you imagined. It means you will receive what you desire—or something better, something aligned with your soul's mission, something that serves your highest good. Even if it doesn't arrive in the form you expect, or at the time you hope for, trust that it is unfolding perfectly. Everything is happening for a reason, orchestrated by a higher intelligence that sees the full picture. You may not understand the reason in this moment, but one day, you will look back and see how every twist and turn was guiding you to where you were meant to be.

If you desire a big house, hold unwavering certainty, not just in the house itself, but in the essence of what it represents: abundance, comfort, expansion. You may receive the exact house, or one even more beautiful, or something similar that fulfills your soul in unexpected ways. And if it doesn't come right now, know that the path is being laid. The Divine timing is precise. You are being led, step by step, to the manifestation that is truly meant for you.

If you desire a soulmate, hold absolute certainty, without any doubt, that you are going to meet them. The person may not look like the one you imagined, nor meet you in the way or place you expected. Certainty doesn't mean becoming fixated on someone specific; it means trusting that everything is unfolding in alignment with your soul's mission. Everything is happening for a reason. If you maintain a positive frequency, you will attract the one who truly belongs to you.

There will be times when you face challenges, defeats, or failures in life. Always remember that the Universe operates in duality; this is known as the Law of Duality, which states that there is always an opposite force. For instance, if you can feel heat, you can also feel cold. Similarly, experiencing sorrow in your life allows you to understand the true meaning of happiness, joy, and peace. If you encounter darkness, it is only then that you can truly recognize light. Success without failure is not possible. However, when you experience failure, remember this vital principle—"Complete Certainty."

If you ask any celebrity or a legend about their life story, or read their biography, you'll find that they faced many failures in the past, like an abusive childhood, poverty, homelessness, betrayals, broken marriages, frauds, scams, etc. And they may still be struggling in certain aspects of their lives. No one is perfect or has everything. Yet, they remain certain beyond logic that life is working for them and through them. Every challenge they face is a test, and every experience teaches them something important for their success. They view everything as part of their experience and believe they will bounce back and succeed.

Whenever things seem to be going wrong, hold onto this "Complete Certainty": It is just a phase that will eventually pass, and you will soon manifest your miracles.

Sometimes we fall again and again, repeating the same mistakes. We put in so much effort, yet it feels like it was all for nothing. We invest deeply in a job or a relationship, but it doesn't materialize the way we hoped. It ends in a layoff or a divorce. It feels like we can never cross the finish line. And then, we start questioning ourselves and our desires about whether they will ever manifest, and doubt whether we made a mistake. But remember, energy is never wasted. No knowledge ever goes to waste. Have "Complete Certainty" that the energy you've created or invested is still there, still working for you. Energy never disappears, and you never lose access to it. All the learning, experience, wisdom, and effort will carry forward into your next job, your next relationship, and your life. Maybe you met someone five years ago, and the deal didn't happen. You never know how the Universe might use that connection in the future to manifest miracles. Everything is unfolding according to a greater plan.

Have unwavering certainty that you will succeed. Nothing is ever truly lost, as long as you don't give up and continue to maintain a high frequency and positive mindset. You only lose that energy when you fall into victimhood, when you believe the world is against you, and let sadness take over. So, bless your failures, rejections, broken relationships, and all the missed opportunities; they are part of your journey, not the end of it. Have "Complete Certainty" in your soul's journey and manifestations

Authenticity

Be authentic! You can only find your true path and pursue your soul's mission when you can fully express yourself without worrying about being judged. When you are free to think and act on your intentions, only then will your Consciousness expand completely.

If you are constantly concerned about other people's opinions or seeking validation and approval, it drains your energy and Consciousness—energy that could be used for more meaningful pursuits. Always stay comfortable in who you are. You can only follow your passion and act on it when you stop caring about what others think. Stop being a people pleaser.

Be confident in your appearance, your looks, your body weight, your clothes, your makeup, and your personality. Yes, strive to live a healthy life and improve yourself as much as possible, but never try to copy someone else or become a "wannabe." Don't dress just to impress others. Wear what makes you feel confident. Only then can you express yourself genuinely, completely, and confidently. You don't need to impress anyone; be your authentic self and be comfortable with it.

All legends dress simply and confidently, caring less about what others might think. They wear clothes that allow them to express their personality and inner self, and what empowers them, what makes them feel good, what lets their intuition shine, and what feels natural to them.

When one feels good, positive, and confident, free from judgment, one can generate high and powerful frequencies that can create miracles in life.

> *Being someone else is the hardest thing to do.*
> *Being yourself is the easiest. Yet, we often choose*
> *the difficult path—due to fear, conditioning, or*
> *a desire to be accepted. We forget that our true*
> *power lies in embracing who we already are.*

Aligned Mindset

> *Your beliefs are your soul's blueprints—they shape your reality, guide your experiences, and reflect the lessons your soul came here to learn.*

Your mindset, perception, and belief system shape the reality you experience. You are not just a participant in your reality; you are its source. Your Consciousness perceives only what it is conditioned to see, and your interactions with others are reflections of your inner world.

Even after death, your beliefs continue to guide your soul's journey. If you believe in Jesus, you'll meet Jesus. If you believe in Krishna, you'll meet Krishna. If you believe in Shiva, you'll find Shiva. If you believe in Allah, you'll find Allah. If you believe in your ancestors, you'll meet them, too. The idea of Heaven and Hell is the result of your guilt or your beliefs about what you deserve. Our belief system shapes not just your life here, but also your journey after death. The afterlife is not a fixed destination; it is a mirror of your belief system.

The same is also mentioned in the Bhagavad Gita: Chapter 9, Verse 25

यान्ति देवव्रता देवान्पितृ न्यान्ति पितृव्रताः |
भूतानि यान्ति भूतेज्या यान्ति मद्याजिनोऽपि माम् ||

yānti deva-vratā devān pitṝn yānti pitṛi-vratāḥ

bhūtāni yānti bhūtejyā yānti mad-yājino 'pi mām

If you worship celestial gods, your soul will go to them. If you worship your ancestors, you'll join them. If you worship spirits or ghosts, you'll be drawn to their realm. But if you worship the Supreme, the ultimate Source, your soul will return to that highest place. Just like water in a pipe can only rise as high as the tank it's connected to, your soul can only rise to the level of the being you worship.

That's why Shree Krishna teaches that to reach the highest spiritual level, we must worship the Supreme, the One, who is eternal, infinite, omnipresent, beyond all forms and names. The Supreme is the Source of everything. Worshipping the Source leads your soul back home.

Free Your Soul from the Karma Matrix

We've been taught for generations that good deeds bring rewards and bad deeds bring suffering in future lives. This belief system, deeply rooted in the idea of Karma and the Cycle of Rebirth (Samsara), creates a mindset that traps the soul in a never-ending loop. It keeps us focused on consequences instead of truth, and binds us to the illusion of separation.

But this cycle is not the ultimate reality—it is part of the Matrix of illusion. It keeps the soul confined, preventing it from returning to its true origin: the Source. Moksha, or liberation, is not something to be earned through endless lifetimes. It is the natural right of every soul, because every soul is already one with the Source. To return, you must free your mind from the belief that you are bound by karma and rebirth. These are illusions that keep you from awakening.

> *You are not here to earn your way back.*
> *You are here to remember you never left.*

Follow the path of Nishkama Karma — which teaches that true salvation—self-realization and freedom from the cycle of rebirth (Samsara)—comes through selfless actions performed without expecting any rewards. Your actions should not be motivated by hopes of gaining something or fears of losing something in future lives. When you let go of the belief that your actions must lead to rewards or punishments in future lives, your soul begins to awaken. It no longer feels the need to return and relive its deeds during the afterlife Life Review process. There is no unfinished business or lingering desire. The soul feels complete. It is free.

And when the soul is complete, it does not seek another birth. Instead, it simply returns to its true home—the Source.

Cheat Code to Manifest Miracles

Don't confuse this all with the Law of Cause and Effect.

The Law of Cause and Effect — applies only within the Matrix. It states that every action will trigger a reaction; every cause will have its corresponding effect, and every deed carries a consequence. Essentially, every seed you sow will yield the same fruits, but this principle operates solely within this Matrix. Once your soul transcends this Matrix, the Law of Cause and Effect no longer applies. However, due to a belief in getting consequences of the deeds, the soul is compelled to return and becomes trapped in the cycle governed by the Law of Cause and Effect.

Every birth is a chance to return to the Source and attain liberation (Moksha). To truly move forward, we must shift our belief system. We need to stop thinking that karma is holding us back or forcing us to return again and again to face the results of our past actions

> *Act with love, not with expectation.*
> *Serve with devotion, not with desire.*
> *This is the way to liberation.*

Atma Karaka: The Soul's Gateway to Liberation

For those familiar with Astrology or who have consulted an astrologer, the concept of the Atma Karaka (AK) holds profound significance. In Jaimini astrology, the Atma

Karaka is the planet with the highest degree in your birth chart. It represents the soul's journey, its deepest desires, and the karmic lessons it must learn in this lifetime.

Many believe that the AK is the planet that brings the greatest suffering and carries the soul's karmic baggage. While this is partially true, it is not the complete picture. The AK is not merely a source of pain — it is also your ticket to liberation.

The Atma Karaka has the power to free your soul from its burdens and guide it back to the Source. It is the planet that can lead you to self-realization and ultimately to Moksha, if you understand its true spiritual purpose.

To awaken and attain enlightenment, one must often pass through suffering and pain. The AK facilitates this process by presenting challenges that act as catalysts for transformation. If you recognize that your suffering is not punishment but a sacred invitation to evolve, you can begin to walk the path of liberation.

The key lies in understanding the nature and significance of your AK planet — its qualities, house placement, and the area of life it influences. Once you identify your AK in your birth chart, begin to act in alignment with its energy through selfless service.

Practice Nishkama Karma — action without attachment to outcomes, rewards, or recognition — especially in the domain governed by your AK. Serve unconditionally, with love and detachment. This spiritual discipline will gradually dissolve karmic patterns, liberate your soul, and help you return to the Source.

↺ Examples of Atma Karaka Planets and Their Spiritual Lessons

☉ Sun as AK

- **Theme:** Ego, leadership, authority, self-identity.

- **Lesson:** Let go of pride and control. Serve with humility. Lead without seeking validation. Learn to collaborate with others—with openness, respect, and shared purpose.

- **Path to Moksha:** Practice selfless leadership and empower others without attachment to recognition. Have a vision to serve humanity and lead others egolessly, focusing on collective upliftment rather than personal glory. Let your light shine not to dominate, but to guide and inspire.

☽ Moon as AK

- **Theme:** Emotions, nurturing, intuition, sensitivity.

- **Lesson:** Transcend emotional dependency and mood fluctuations. Learn emotional detachment with compassion. Learn to take control of your thoughts and subconscious mind.

- **Path to Moksha:** Nurture others selflessly, offering care and support without expecting emotional reciprocation. Develop emotional resilience, learning to stay centered through life's emotional tides. Trust your inner guidance without fear or the need for approval — let your intuition be your compass. Allow your emotional depth to become a source of healing for others, not a source of attachment.

♀ Venus as AK

- **Theme:** Love, art, creativity, beauty, relationships, pleasure.

- **Lesson:** Transcend attachment to sensual pleasures and romantic ideals. Recognize that creativity is the ultimate power—the sacred force through which you live your true life.

- **Path to Moksha:** Offer unconditional love and devotion, without expectations or emotional entanglement. Create beauty that uplifts others, whether through art, creativity, kindness, or presence. Detach from emotional dependencies, allowing love to flow freely without control or need. Let your relationships become a reflection of divine love — pure, expansive, and liberating. Find joy in uplifting others.

♃ Jupiter as AK

- **Theme:** Wisdom, expansion, spirituality, dharma.

- **Lesson:** Go beyond intellectual pride and spiritual superiority. Live your teachings with humility and authenticity. Understand that dharma is deeply personal—and truth, when lived, becomes your true dharma.

- **Path to Moksha:** Share your knowledge selflessly, without seeking admiration or authority. Guide others with compassion, becoming a beacon of wisdom and kindness. Walk the path of dharma with humility, living your truth and uplifting others through your example. Let your spiritual journey be a service to humanity, not a pursuit of status.

♄ **Saturn as AK**

- **Theme:** Discipline, responsibility, suffering, karma.

- **Lesson:** Embrace hardship as a teacher. Cultivate patience, endurance, and a spirit of service toward the underprivileged. Recognize that life is not always fair—but it always offers opportunities for growth.

- **Path to Moksha:** Serve diligently, even when the path is slow or difficult. Accept delays and limitations gracefully, recognizing them as part of your soul's purification. Act with integrity and serve your employer or duties without attachment to recognition or rewards. Let your work become a form of spiritual offering, grounded in humility and perseverance.

☿ **Mercury as AK**

- **Theme:** Intellect, communication, learning, curiosity, problem solving skills.

- **Lesson:** Move beyond superficial knowledge and ego-driven intellect. Speak your truth with wisdom, and make decisions with maturity and clarity.

- **Path to Moksha:** Share wisdom selflessly, without seeking praise or superiority. Communicate with compassion, using your words to heal, guide, and uplift. Use your problem-solving skills to help others selflessly, without attachment to the outcome or rewards. Let your intellect become a tool for service, not self-importance — a bridge between minds and hearts.

♂ Mars as AK

- **Theme:** Action, courage, aggression, ambition, desires.

- **Lesson:** Transform impulsiveness into purposeful action. Channel energy into service, not domination. Master your anger and desires, allowing inner peace to guide your choices.

- **Path to Moksha:** Act with courage for the greater good, not for personal glory. Protect others, stand up for truth, and fight injustice without seeking rewards or validation. Don't look for recognition for every act of bravery — let your strength be a silent offering to the divine. Channel your energy into service-driven action, where the motive is love, not ego.

Desires are the threads that bind us to the Matrix. Each desire—whether grand or subtle—leaves an imprint on the soul and shapes our belief system. These imprints draw us back into the cycle of birth and rebirth, just so we

Cheat Code to Manifest Miracles

can fulfill those desires. We return again and again, drawn by the pull of unfulfilled longings.

To be free, we must let go of all desires—whether they are big or small—and also release ourselves from concepts like sin, virtue, merit, heaven, hell, remorse, and even karma. These ideas are part of the Matrix in which we live, and they keep us bound to illusion.

Ultimately, establish the following belief system: This life—this Matrix—is all we have while we are here. It operates under its own Law of Cause and Effect. Whatever actions we take, whether good or bad, we experience the consequences in this life itself. Once our physical form, or avatar, dies, the soul is no longer bound by this Matrix. It becomes free and begins its journey back to the Source. When the soul is free from belief systems like remorse, sin, virtue, merit, desires, or karma, it no longer feels bound by them during the afterlife Life Review process. Without these mental and emotional imprints, the soul is not trapped or pulled back into the cycle of rebirth. Instead, it remains clear, light, and free, ready to return to the Source.

> *Free your mind,*
> *and you will free*
> *yourself from the Matrix.*

Open all our senses and understand that whatever happens in your reality is a creation of your mind and Consciousness. Your mind is interconnected with the Universal Mind, the source of everything that has created this Simulation. In turn, all of our minds are connected to the Universal Mind of the Source. Therefore, we are all connected through our minds.

This concept was also supported by the scientists who won the Nobel Prize in Physics in 2022, as they provided evidence for the Entanglement Theory. In simple terms, this theory suggests that two atoms that were once connected will always remain connected, regardless of the distance between them. We can relate this to our everyday lives. Two people who were once close can still feel connected even when miles apart. For example, when one person thinks about the other, they may find that the second person is also thinking of them at the same time. You might have experienced this when you think of someone and then receive a call from them later that day or the next. Or perhaps you mention that you were missing someone, and they respond by saying they were missing you, too.

Similarly, you might crave a specific food, and your spouse surprises you by cooking it or bringing it home. We have all heard stories about a mother sensing when her child is in danger, or we can sense when something is wrong with our loved ones. We often refer to these experiences as coincidences or intuition. However, all of this occurs because our minds and Consciousness are part of the same source, and we are all connected.

Use this connection to your benefit and create miracles in your life. Learn and practice telepathy, and you will be

Cheat Code to Manifest Miracles

able to transmit your thoughts to others without the need to call them.

Unconditional Love

The Divine Matrix, or the Simulation we live in, has a purpose. The purpose is to evolve our soul toward unconditional love. Unconditional love is a power that no one can resist, and it comes with our ability to be non-judgmental. Even God, or the Creator, cannot resist the force of unconditional love. However, you must leave all your judgments behind for this. Accept others as they are and yourself as you are.

> *Unconditional love is the highest frequency of creation. It asks for nothing, expects nothing, and yet transforms everything.*

We often try to humanize God by applying the same rules and protocols that society imposes on us—but God is beyond all human attributes.

God is eternal, infinite, formless, nameless, and omnipresent.

God is neither a man nor a woman; God has no gender.

The term "Unconditional Love" is the closest we can come to describing God. Anything that motivates you to hate, judge, or separate from others cannot be aligned with God—who is the One, the Source, the Creator of all.

When we judge something or someone, we invite the same tests and challenges into our lives so that we can learn from them. For instance, if you judge someone for their body shape or being overweight, your metabolism slows down immediately, and you start putting on weight.

We've all seen moments—either in our own lives or in the lives of others—where judgment comes full circle. Someone may strongly criticize extramarital affairs, only to later discover that their own partner is involved in one, or they unexpectedly find themselves in a similar situation. Sometimes, we judge someone in the morning or gossip about them, and by evening, we become the subject of gossip or criticism ourselves. You might argue with someone early in the day, and by the time you return home, you're in a deeper conflict with your spouse.

These experiences are not coincidences. They are mirrors—reflections of our own energy, thoughts, and judgments. Life has a way of showing us what we project. It teaches us not through punishment, but through reflection. It is actually our Consciousness contracting, telling us to learn the same lesson so that we can grow in unconditional love without judgment. Therefore, unconditional love without judgment for yourself, humanity, and everyone is very important. This is the only thing that you will find in the heavens when you crossover and go back to the Source after leaving this Simulation.

Every soul goes through a Life Review after leaving this world. In this process, you are not judged by others; you

   Cheat Code to Manifest Miracles

are judged by your own soul to reflect on how you treated people during your time in this Simulation. You will meet everyone you interacted with in the Matrix. The most challenging part is revisiting moments where you caused harm, pain, or tried to control others. Therefore, practice unconditional love without judgment and forgiveness as much as possible if you truly want to manifest miracles in your lives. Any aspect of ourselves or others that we judge will contract our Consciousness and block our ability to manifest miracles in our lives.

True love is never conditional. If you are seeking love that is based on conditions, remember—the Universe will reflect the same in your life. You will attract people who place conditions on you and try to control you. If your love depends on someone fulfilling your expectations, it's not love—it's a transaction, a conditional agreement. Love that fades when needs aren't met was never love to begin with. Conditional love is rooted in ego, identity, and attachment.

But when you transcend the boundaries of ego, beliefs, gender, body, needs, and culture, when you dissolve into pure Consciousness, you become the embodiment of unconditional love. Divine Consciousness is unconditional love. It does not ask, demand, or expect. It simply is— radiant, infinite, and free.

Love Yourself First – Learn to love yourself unconditionally, just as you would love someone else. Show yourself the same empathy, care, and respect that you seek from others or that you freely give to them. If you're currently single or not in a relationship, remind yourself:

"Who cares? I am here for myself. I choose to love myself unconditionally."

The one person you should actively seek, find, and promise to be married to until death—is yourself.

When you love yourself in this way, you naturally attract others who resonate with that positive energy. Waiting to receive love from others is an illusion—just another aspect of the Matrix. The truth is that you must love yourself first. That's the fundamental rule of this Matrix.

Anything you try to manifest solely for yourself, or your ego will take much longer to materialize—and even if it does, you may struggle to sustain it. Instead, manifest with a higher purpose—for the people around you, your community, your country, the world, and the Universe.

Manifest with the power of unconditional love, and for the highest good of all.

Thriving in the Era of AI: The Power of Human Consciousness

In the age of artificial intelligence and tools like ChatGPT, one fundamental element that remains absent from AI is Consciousness. As of today, AI does not possess Consciousness or emotions. It can simulate conversation, analyze data, and even mimic creativity and sympathy, but it lacks authenticity, intuition, and the capacity for unconditional love.

Numerous UFO researchers and witnesses have reported seeing UFOs built from a material that exhibits signs of Consciousness. These accounts suggest a future where technology might integrate conscious elements. However, until such breakthroughs occur in our daily lives, it is safe to say that AI remains a powerful tool but not a sentient one.

What sets us apart as humans is our innate Consciousness. We are capable of deep emotional connection, intuitive insight, and the electromagnetic power of the heart. We are capable of loving unconditionally and acting authentically, and we navigate life with a sense of purpose that no algorithm can replicate. As AI continues to evolve, it will inevitably transform industries, replacing roles in industries like IT, Medicine, Research, Education, the Creative Arts, and even Astrology. But this shift shouldn't diminish our value. Instead, it calls us to lean into what makes us uniquely human. In this new era, our heart-centered intelligence, authenticity, unconditional love, and intuition will be our greatest assets. These qualities will not only help us adapt but also allow us to thrive, creating meaning, connection, and innovation that AI alone cannot achieve.

Let me share a personal example. I am an astrologer. When I read a horoscope or kundli, I analyze ten to fifteen yogas or planetary conjunctions. I examine the major period (Mahadasha) and the minor period (Antardasha) currently influencing the concerned individual. I may also refer to two or three divisional charts to answer specific questions. Based on this, I offer insights into a person's life and future. But in the coming years, AI-powered astrology apps will be able to do much more. They will scan hundreds of yogas and conjunctions, interpret all layers of planetary periods: Mahadasha, Antardasha, Pratyantar Dasha, Sukshma Dasha, with precision, and read every divisional chart in detail. Their predictions may even surpass mine in technical accuracy.

Yet, there is one thing AI cannot replicate: intuition. My ability to read a chart is not just based on data; it's guided by Divine grace, inner knowing, a deep connection to the Source, and the unique energy of each individual. This intuitive wisdom allows me to interpret the chart in a way that resonates with their life's journey.

This principle applies to every profession, whether you're in IT, Medicine, Education, or the Creative Arts. AI will become more capable, more efficient, and more widespread. But what will always set us apart is our Consciousness, our emotional intelligence, and our intuitive insight.

To thrive in the era of AI, we must evolve not just technologically, but spiritually and emotionally. We must cultivate the human qualities that machines cannot replicate, like love, empathy, authenticity, intuition, and the wisdom of the heart.

CHAPTER 8

Simple Shifting to a New Parallel Reality

> *Our greatest power is the power to choose. Through this power, you can shift to a new and better reality. This is the true free will given to each one of us in this Simulation.*

There are an infinite number of possible and parallel realities for you and for everyone else. All these realities overlap and coexist simultaneously. The past, present, and future all exist within you, and they're happening at the same time. We often think time moves in a straight line, just like walking on a road feels linear. But we forget that the Earth is round. You can start walking east and eventually return to the same point from the west. If we could see ourselves from a higher plane, we'd realize we're actually moving in a circular motion. In the same way, time only appears linear from our limited perspective. From higher dimensions, everything—past, present, and future—is happening all at once. It's all connected. You simply don't have the vision yet to see your entire soul journey unfolding at once.

When you change yourself in the present, it alters your future, and when the future changes, it also reshapes the past. Everything is interconnected and exists in relation to one another.

Every thought, action, and decision creates a new parallel reality. The key is to become aware of which reality you want to experience and how to shift into the one you desire. We are constantly shifting between these realities by changing the focus of our Consciousness.

Consciousness simply means awareness with a choice. Think of your Consciousness as a camera lens through which you're filming your life—your reality. This lens captures each moment as a frame, and these frames string together to create the video of your current timeline. Wherever the lens focuses, that's the frame you generate. And frame by frame, you're creating your reality.

Editing the Frames of Your Life

We often think of life as a continuous stream of events, but in truth, it's a collection of moments—like still frames in a video. Just as a video editor selects, enhances, or removes frames to shape a compelling story, we too have the power to edit our life's timeline by consciously choosing where to focus our awareness.

When we go on vacation, we take dozens of pictures. Later, we select the best ones, add music, and create a reel that tells a story. The reel isn't just a random collection—it's a curated experience. Similarly, our life is a reel of emotional, mental, and spiritual snapshots. The music we add is our emotional tone. The frames we choose to highlight become our reality.

What Is a Life Frame?

A life frame is a moment—a thought, a memory, a feeling, a decision. It's a snapshot of your consciousness at a specific point in time. These frames, when strung together, create your life's narrative.

Editing Your Life Frames

To change your life, you don't need to rewrite the entire story. You just need to edit the frames that no longer serve you. Here are some examples:

- **Reframing Painful Memories**

  A childhood experience that once brought shame can be revisited with compassion. Instead of seeing it as a wound, you can view it as a soul-chosen lesson for growth. This shift in perception edits the emotional tone of that frame.

- **Replacing Limiting Thoughts**

  If you constantly think, "I'm not good enough," that thought becomes a recurring frame. By consciously replacing it with, "I am worthy and evolving," you begin to change the storyline of your life.

- **Shifting Relationship Dynamics**

  A toxic relationship may be a frame that repeats itself. Editing it might mean setting boundaries, expressing your truth, or choosing to walk away. This act of courage rewrites the emotional tone of your journey.

- **Transforming Daily Habits**

  If your routine feels stagnant, insert new frames: moments of gratitude, creativity, or silence. These small edits shift the rhythm of your life reel.

Wherever your lens focuses, that's the frame you generate. If you focus on lack, you create frames of scarcity. If you focus on love, you create frames of abundance. Your Consciousness is the camera lens. Your awareness is the editor. You are not just the actor in your life—you are the director, the editor, and the visionary. The Universe responds to your edits. When you consciously choose your thoughts, emotions, and intentions, you begin to manifest a reality that reflects your awakened state.

So, never forget that in the video of your life journey, the camera lens is your Consciousness. It's what ultimately produces the timeline of your life. If you want to change

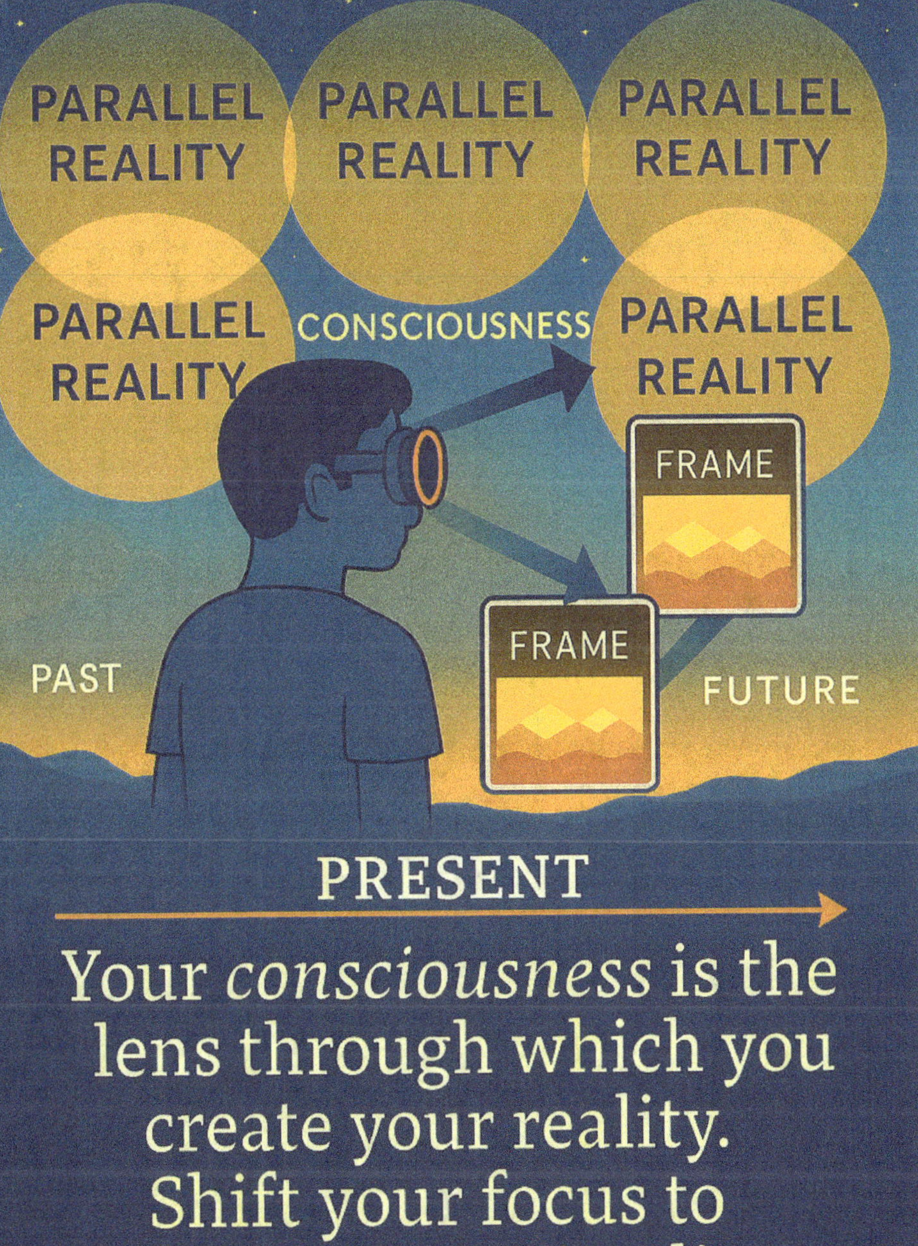

Your *consciousness* is the lens through which you create your reality. Shift your focus to change your timeline.

Your Emotional State
sets the Frequency.
Your Choice tunes
the Reality.

your reality, you must first change the frame that's creating that timeline. To do that, you need to shift the focus of your lens—that is, your Consciousness. Only then can you begin to experience a shift in your reality, one that aligns with your highest intentions and inner truth.

> *Your Consciousness is the lens through which you create your reality. Shift your focus to change your timeline.*

Now that you understand that shifting your current reality requires shifting the focus of your Consciousness, the next question that may arise is:

How do you change the focus of your Consciousness?

As we explored earlier, the universe acts as a mirror. You can shift your Consciousness by changing your thoughts, feelings, emotions, behaviors, perceptions, and your overall frequency.

At any given moment, you have a choice. You can choose to frown and become angry, which will shift you into a parallel reality where the world reflects that anger back at you. You'll find yourself on a timeline where everything and everyone seems to provoke frustration or sadness. In doing so, you're essentially downgrading your reality from a positive one to a negative one. Or, you can choose to smile, feel grateful, and carry yourself like someone who is truly blessed. This choice shifts you into a more positive, elevated version of reality, a new and improved timeline.

At any moment, you have the power to upgrade or downgrade your reality. The choice is always yours—and that choice is your free will.

Therefore, to upgrade your reality and shift the focus of your Consciousness, you must consciously choose to remain in a positive and high-frequency state. Avoid giving your attention and energy to anything that lowers your frequency—such as stress and negative emotions.

Parallel realities can be understood like choosing a TV channel. When you want to watch something on TV, your mood—how you feel and what you're thinking—helps you decide what kind of program to watch. If you're happy, you might choose a comedy or something entertaining or fun. If you're feeling emotional, maybe you'll go for sad songs or a romantic series. If you're curious, you might pick a documentary or a supernatural movie.

So, your emotional state sets your frequency, and that frequency guides your choice of channel. Out of all the channels available, you pick one—and that program starts playing. But that doesn't mean the other channels stop existing. They're all still there, broadcasting at the same time.

Life works the same way. All possibilities exist at once. Your emotional state is like the remote control; it sets

Cheat Code to Manifest Miracles

your frequency, and that frequency decides which version of reality you experience.

You get to choose what plays on your screen.

Free Will vs Destiny

I'm often asked this question, especially since I'm also an astrologer and have seen how accurately Astrology can reflect people's lives:

Do we truly have free will to change our destiny, or is everything already predetermined?

What role does free will play in a life that seems so destined?

Before you were born, your soul chose a life path—filled with specific experiences and challenges. This choice was made with free will, and it became the destiny of your physical self—your avatar in this lifetime.

It feels like destiny because your physical self doesn't remember that, as a soul, you agreed to this path. But even though the path is chosen, you still have freedom in how you walk it.

You can choose:

- *How fast or slow you move through your journey*
- *How deeply you engage with your purpose*
- *How many lives you touch—just a few, thousands, or even millions*

- *How you express your gifts, face your challenges, and grow*

Your life path is flexible. It expands or contracts based on the choices you make. The more willing you are to engage with your journey, the faster you evolve, the more you achieve, and the greater your impact. If you resist or slow down, the journey may take longer—but you'll still face the lessons your soul set up for you, in one form or another.

> *Destiny is the map. Free will is how you travel. The soul chose the path, but you choose the pace.*

Walking the Hallway of Destiny

Imagine walking down a long hallway. This hallway represents your destiny—your soul's chosen life path. Before you incarnated, your soul laid out this path with intention and purpose. But how you walk it is entirely up to you. You can choose to walk, run, crawl, or even fly. You can move through it with joy or sorrow. You can pause and explore every door along the way, or ignore them all. You can meet people and leave a trail of love and light—or choose conflict and resistance. You can take breaks, engage in distractions, or elevate yourself through conscious choices.

You can walk this hallway however you wish. You can move forward with grace, or keep returning to the same point until the lesson is learned. You can walk upside down, or ride through it in luxury. But one truth remains: you will walk it. Because walking this hallway is the free will of your soul. It chose this journey for a reason—an experience meant to stretch, evolve, and awaken your soul.

There's no need to resist the hallway. It's already written. But your actions, choices, and attitude shape the experience of walking it.

So ask yourself:

- *Do you want to walk it joyfully, creating positive experiences for yourself and or others?*
- *Or forcefully and painfully, surrounded by negativity?*

> *The hallway is yours. The life path and journey are sacred—laid out by your soul for a reason. And every step you take is a reflection of your soul's evolution.*

Your Reality Is a Choice

Imagine walking into a multiplex cinema where many movies are playing at the same time in different auditoriums.

You walk into Auditorium 1 and start watching a movie. The film is already made—the script is written, the actors are performing their roles, and everything is playing out as planned. If you don't like the movie, you can't change what's on the screen, because it's already been created. But here's the important part: you can choose to leave.

You can walk into Auditorium 2, where a different movie is playing—maybe one with a better story, stronger characters, or a message that feels more aligned with you. Or you might walk into Auditorium 3, where the movie is darker, the characters are stuck in loops, and the lead character (you) is stressed and unhappy.

That simple act of switching auditoriums is your free will in action. It's your power to upgrade or downgrade your reality.

Life works the same way. All possibilities—like all movies—exist at the same time. Your conscious choice decides which one you experience. You're never stuck. You always have the power to shift your reality by choosing a different "movie" to watch.

   Cheat Code to Manifest Miracles

A Simple Practice to Shift Your Reality Using Free Will

Exercise 8.1: Try this small yet powerful exercise to experience how your free will can reshape your reality.

One day, upon waking, make a conscious decision:

No matter what happens today, I will not be angry or react to any negative situation. I will not seek instant gratification, nor will I respond impulsively to anything or anyone.

Instead, choose to

- focus your thoughts on positivity and possibility
- spend time only with friends who uplift and motivate you
- eat nourishing, healthy food that supports your well-being
- visualize your goals with clarity and intention
- stay calm and composed, refusing to lose your temper over anything
- pause before speaking, and ask yourself, "Is what I'm about to say healthy, true, and aligned with my highest self? What will be the consequences if these words manifest as reality?"
- throughout the day, remain in a state of gratitude, for the blessings you already have and for those that are on their way as your desires begin to manifest
- walk as if you are blessed, speak as if you are blessed, and act like a blessed person; you are deserving of all the love and success in the world.

At the end of the day, review your experiences. Reflect on how many troubles, conflicts, and emotional disturbances you avoided simply by shifting your attitude and exercising your free will. This is how you step into a new, positive reality by consciously choosing your responses, your focus, and your energy.

Each person experiences their own unique reality shaped by their perceptions of themselves, others, and their circumstances. I am the producer, writer, actor, and director of my own choices and experiences, and you exist in my reality as I perceive you. I might see you as bad, selfish, evil, or unkind, even if you are a wonderful person in your own reality. For me, you are what I perceive, regardless of how others see you.

On the other hand, you might be an angel, a guru, or a deeply inspiring figure in my reality, while in someone else's, you could be seen as a criminal, a manipulator, a murderer, a rapist, or even worse. Just look at the many recently prosecuted gurus, celebrities, or business tycoons around the world. While their followers saw them as Divine or God-like, others saw them as deeply flawed or even dangerous. This illustrates a powerful truth:

> *You are not responsible for how others perceive you in their reality, and you cannot control that.*

Beyond individual realities, there is also a collective reality, a shared timeline that emerges from the co-creation of all our individual experiences. This collective creation forms a country's timeline, then a global timeline, which we often refer to as a Yuga (era), and ultimately, the timeline of the Universe itself. This idea will lead us to the theory of the multiverse, a concept I will explore further in my next book. For now, understand the following:

> *Every choice you make shifts your reality—moment by moment, frame by frame. With each decision, you're shaping the path you're walking.*

CHAPTER 9

How to Create a Miracle

> **Miracles are glitches in the Matrix, unfolding at any moment. They are Divine messages reminding us that reality is fluid, time and space are illusions, and the impossible is often just a shift in perception away.**

First, we need to understand what miracles truly are. Miracles are anomalies that occur within the Divine Matrix or Quantum Field, which we also know as illusion or Maya. These are not expected or anticipated through the usual paths and choices. The likelihood of a miracle occurring by simply following routine patterns is extremely low or negligible. In essence, a miracle is anything that cannot be explained by natural or logical means. That's why miracles are often seen as supernatural events or signs of Divine intervention.

Whether it's Quantum Physics, Astrology, or any other occult or Divine science, none of these disciplines predict a single, fixed outcome for any observation. Instead, they predict multiple possibilities, each with its own likelihood of occurring. Now, consider the following: When we change our choices or deviate from our usual patterns, we open the door to new possibilities. What once seemed impossible can suddenly become real. This shift in perception is what we often refer to as a miracle or a glitch in the Quantum Field.

Miracles are not bound by logic or routine. They are anomalies within the Divine Matrix, or Maya, that defy expectation. They occur when we align with a higher frequency, step outside the predictable, and allow Divine Consciousness to intervene.

A Knock at Midnight – A True Miracle Story of Faith and Divine Timing

My father often shares a story from a time before I was born. He worked for the government, and my mother was a schoolteacher. After years of saving, they decided to buy a piece of land to build our family home.

After much searching, they found a property they loved. Everything was agreed upon verbally with the seller, who promised to finalize the registration in a few days. My parents needed some time anyway to gather the funds by liquidating some of their assets.

But one night, the seller called unexpectedly. He told my parents that another buyer had offered a higher price and was ready to complete the registration the very next day. Unless my father could match the offer and pay immediately, the land would be sold to someone else.

It was heartbreaking and deeply unfair. My parents tried everything they could to arrange for the extra money by that evening, but they still fell short by a few thousand rupees. After dinner, they sat together and discussed the land and what else they could do to obtain the funds by morning. But they didn't feel discouraged, and neither did they start yelling, crying, or cursing the seller. They surrendered to God, realizing they might lose the land they had dreamed of building their home on.

Around midnight, the doorbell rang at their rented house. My father opened the door to find a man he didn't immediately recognize. The man introduced himself and reminded my father of a time, years ago, when he was a young college graduate preparing for a government job. He had no money to even submit the application or pay for the training. My father had helped him back then, covering both the application and training fees.

That night, the man handed my father the exact amount they were short of, without being asked, and said that he had to catch a bus back to his hometown. He left as quickly as he arrived. My parents were stunned. It had been years since my father had helped him, and he had never expected the money to be returned. It was a moment of pure joy, gratitude, and awe—a true miracle.

This story has stayed with me as a powerful reminder:

> *When you truly desire something and focus on it with unwavering belief and positive intention, the Universe responds.*

If you know what you want to manifest, hold that vision with complete certainty, and surrender the rest to the Creator. Miracles occur when faith aligns with intention.

Our perceptions shape our experiences. If you believe in miracles and expect them, they will manifest. If you believe life is hard, people are cruel, and miracles don't exist, then that becomes your reality. Remember, the Universe is a giant mirror—it reflects your beliefs back to you. But when you realize that it's all an illusion, that everything is happening for you, through you, you begin to understand that these experiences are part of the Divine Matrix. You came here to learn, grow, and evolve. Nothing is happening against you. No soul is inherently evil. What we perceive as "good" or "bad" is simply the behavior of the avatar, the temporary personality and identity that a soul adopts within this Matrix. These actions, whether noble or misguided, are part of the soul's journey to learn, grow, and evolve.

Miracles happen when you learn to manipulate the energy of this Matrix and discover how to create with it. Just as the purpose of any simulator is to facilitate learning, we are not here to escape the Matrix; we are here to understand it and learn from it.

The Matrix often tries to distract you with things that don't truly matter, such as politics, loans, criticism, toxic relationships, debts, expensive cars, fake happiness, luxury items, and endless bills. It can also fill your mind with uncontrollable thoughts, including:

- "What do people think of me?"
- "Why don't they like me?"
- "Why are others more successful?"
- "Why do they have what I don't?"
- "Why are they so happy, while I am not?"
- "Why are they so wealthy, while I am not?"

These thoughts and worries can keep you stuck and block your ability to manifest what you genuinely desire. To create the life you want, you need to focus your energy on what truly matters. Let go of distractions and stay connected to your Higher Self. That's when real miracles begin to happen.

You are not what you think you are;
you are so much more!

You are like angels who have forgotten their powers, walking this planet to experience all that life has to offer, so you may remember your true essence. The miracle code lies within you, within your body, guiding you toward your superpower.

To create a miracle, I'm going to share a powerful cheat code you can apply daily until your miracle manifests. And once it does, continue practicing it to sustain your miracle and enter a reality where miracles become a part of your everyday life. They won't just be one-time events anymore. They'll become inevitable.

This cheat code is divided into two parts, and it's important to master both parts to manifest a miracle in your life.

Cheat Code Part 1: The Calm, Non-Reactive State

This is the foundation of all the miracles that happen around us. To create miracles, you must first master your inner world. This state aligns you with clarity, intuition, and higher frequencies. No matter what's happening around you, maintain inner peace. Don't react negatively to any situation that is happening around you immediately. Always pause before responding.

Anything you do, say, or even think that stems from lack or fear is reactive. This reactive energy disconnects you from the Source, the Divine Consciousness—the very force that manifests miracles. No matter how right an action may seem, if it arises from a reactive state, it won't work out the way you hope. Even the "right" thing, when done reactively, becomes the wrong thing. Before replying to a message or

  Cheat Code to Manifest Miracles

making a decision while feeling upset, anxious, or triggered, take a pause. First, become completely calm, peaceful, whole within, and indifferent to the outcome. Let peace settle in your heart. Only then should you take action.

When you find yourself in a situation where you don't know what's right or wrong, don't rush. Instead, choose to act like the Divine Consciousness—from a place of peace, clarity, and inner strength. Detach from the drama and practice silence. Stay calm. That's when your actions will truly align with the energy of miracles.

> *God's mind or Divine Consciousness resides*
> *in a calm, still, and non-reactive state.*
> *It is found in Silence. Breathe. Be Still. Listen.*

Follow these two steps to achieve this calm and non-reactive state:

- **Step 1: The Power of Stillness**

No matter what is happening around you, choose to remain calm. When something goes wrong, resist the urge to react immediately. Instead, pause. Breathe. Reflect. Remind yourself,

> *This is not happening to me;*
> *this is happening for me.*

Every challenge you face is an experience that your soul has chosen for growth. Everything happens for a reason, even if you don't understand it at the moment. In the future, you will look back and realize why it all happened. Every test and situation in your life has been meticulously planned by your soul to facilitate your learning. Recognize that whenever a problem arises, you are the common factor in all these situations. It is you who has chosen to go through these experiences. When you acknowledge this, you begin to reclaim your power.

> *The one constant in all your life problems is you.*
> *Shift your awareness to stillness and calmness, and*
> *the problems begin to dissolve.*

- **Step 2: The Prayer That Heals**

In moments of stress or conflict, take a sacred pause and silently repeat this powerful mantra to your soul:

> *I love you. I am sorry.*
> *Please forgive me. Thank you.*

This is called the Ho'oponopono prayer, a traditional Hawaiian practice of healing and reconciliation. It is important to note that this mantra is not my original creation—it is part of an ancient cultural tradition.

Ho'oponopono is an ancient Hawaiian practice of making things right and is more than just a prayer; it's a cultural process that has been passed down through generations. It is a prayer of taking responsibility for things happening around you, cleansing, and releasing any karma. It purifies your emotional and mental space, dissolving the energetic residue of past experiences that trigger negative reactions.

Why Calmness is the Ultimate Power

When you are calm, you align with clarity, intuition, and higher frequencies. Calmness is not weakness; it is mastery. When you embody this state consistently, you become a magnet for miracles. You are no longer resisting life; you are flowing with it. And in that flow, the Universe conspires to support you.

As told by Sri Ramana Maharshi,

- In perfect calm, time stops
- Karma pauses
- Samskaras (impressions from past experiences) dissolve
- Everything becomes still, and in that stillness, transformation begins.

Miracles happen when we learn our life lessons without having to go through the pain and suffering that often comes with the challenges our soul has chosen for us.

There are two paths to soul growth: We can either confront the challenges we face, experience suffering, and eventually learn from those painful events, or we can choose to bypass the suffering and simply absorb the lessons without undergoing a painful transformation by entering a calm and non-reactive state. Understand that life is like a game in which everyone plays a role in your story. By adopting this mindset, you can skip the suffering and just learn the lessons. When you recognize that the events occurring in your life are meant for your growth, rather than seeing them as conspiracies against you, you gain the power to change your narrative by maintaining that calm, non-reactive state.

For example, if you deeply love someone and marry them, believing that you are now settled for life, only to discover that they betray you, this betrayal serves as a challenge preplanned by your soul to help you experience and learn from it. If you react with anger and frustration, your suffering will only increase, and you will ultimately learn the lesson after enduring considerable pain. However, you can choose to learn the lesson without suffering by maintaining that calm and non-reactive state.

Understand that no soul owns another; therefore, no one is truly possessive of anyone else. This shift in perspective can lead to a miracle in your life. It's your reality, so you have the choice to either forgive the person or separate from them. Always strive to make decisions from a calm and non-reactive place. Ultimately, this is your movie. You are the director, and everyone else is a character in your narrative.

Always remember, the more you try to control others' reality or the outcome of their movie, the more it slips away from your hands. But when you surrender control

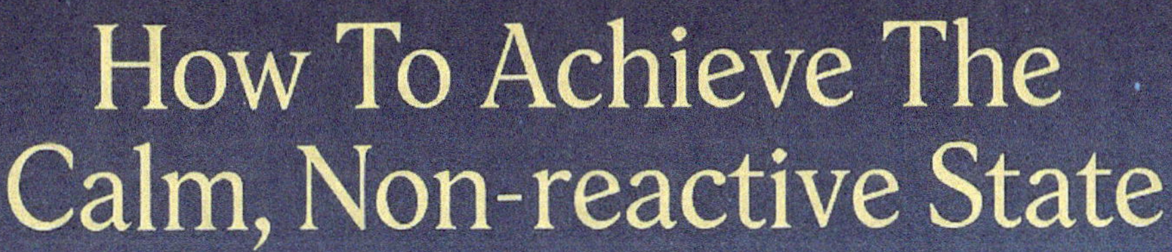

How To Achieve The Calm, Non-reactive State

- Pause Before Reacting

- Use the Healing Prayer, "I love you. I am sorry. Please forgive me. Thank you."

- Understand Everything is Happening for Me

- Have Complete Certainty

- Feel the Calmness and Stillness inside you

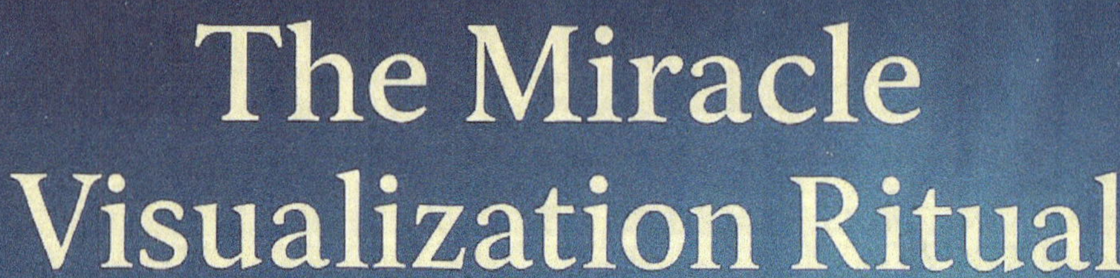

Crystal Clear Goal

Enter a Calm State

Activate the Heart's Power

Visualize Your Miracle

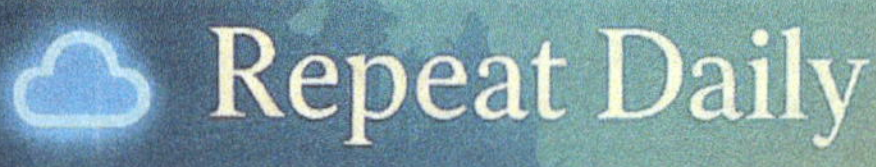

Repeat Daily

and choose a calm and non-reactive state, you transform your reality.

Cheat Code Part 2: The Miracle Visualization Ritual

Once you've mastered the calm, non-reactive state, you're ready to activate the second part of the cheat code. Begin with absolute faith. Believe, without a shadow of doubt, that your miracle will manifest. Let go of the "how" and "when." The outcome is not in your hands, and that's okay. Your job is to align your energy, not control the process.

The Power of the Heart's Electromagnetic Field

Science has revealed something truly extraordinary: The heart's electromagnetic field is thousands of times more powerful than that of the brain. Unlike the brain's field, the heart's electromagnetic signature can be detected several feet outside the body, influencing not only our internal systems but also the energetic environment around us. This powerful field plays a vital role in energetic communication and allows us to connect with others and the Universe on a deeper, more intuitive level. When we activate the power of our heart, especially during meditation or visualization, we awaken our Divine spark that connects us with the Source, the Divine Consciousness, and we tap into a source of wisdom and guidance that transcends logic and thought.

The brain can be seen as a spiritual antenna, tuning us into the frequency of this third-dimensional reality. It constantly translates subtle vibrations into tangible experiences, converting imagination into physical form. Acting as an interface, the brain interprets our thoughts and inner visions, shaping them into the material world we perceive. The heart, however, is the tuning dial. Like adjusting a radio to the right station, the heart allows us to align with the wavelength of Source Consciousness. It is through the heart that we receive Divine communication, intuitive guidance, and soul-level knowing. While the brain decodes the external, the heart connects us to the eternal.

Source Consciousness resides within the heart. When we open our hearts—truly and vulnerably—we create a direct channel to the Divine. In this sacred space, we move beyond thought and into pure presence, where miracles unfold and truth is felt rather than understood.

The heart is not just a physical organ; it is a spiritual gateway. It is through the heart that our Consciousness communicates with the Higher Self, Spirit Guides, and Divine energies. Our heart is a key to human freedom. The wisdom of the heart can beat the programming of our mind and of this Matrix. If our body is our temple, then the heart is the innermost sacred sanctuary, or in Hinduism, we call it "Garbhgrah" of the temple. By aligning with the heart's frequency, we amplify our ability to manifest, heal, and connect with the miraculous.

Therefore, for this visualization technique, we will use the electromagnetic power of our heart.

> *Quiet the mind,*
> *open the heart—this is where Source speaks.*

1. **Be Crystal Clear:** *Define exactly what you want to manifest. Be specific. The clearer your vision, the stronger your signal to the Universe.*

2. **Enter a Calm State:** *Close your eyes gently. Take a few deep, slow breaths. With each exhale, relax your body—starting from your feet and moving upward to the crown of your head.*

   – *Allow thoughts to come and go like passing clouds. Don't resist or engage with them. Simply observe without reaction. Your goal is to enter a state of inner stillness and silence.*

   – *If a thought persists, softly repeat the keyword "Stop" three (3) times. This keyword acts as a gentle command to quiet the mind.*

   – *Continue repeating "Stop" whenever needed, until you reach a still, calm, thoughtless, and non-reactive state of being.*

3. **Activate the Heart's Power:** *Gently place your hand over your heart to guide yourself where to focus your attention. This simple act activates the heart's energy field.*

4. **Visualize Your Miracle:** *Now, begin to visualize your desire as already fulfilled.*

   – *Use your childlike imagination to experience it in vivid detail, the sights, sounds, colors, and most importantly, the emotions.*

> — *Feel the joy, gratitude, and excitement; bring all the emotions, even tears of joy and happiness, as if it's happening now.*
>
> — *Visualize how your miracle is not only transforming your life but also positively impacting others.*
>
> — *Say 'Thank You' with a heart full of gratitude, slowly bring your awareness back, and gently come out of the meditation.*
>
> 5. ***Repeat Daily:*** *Practice this visualization twice a day, once in the morning as you wake up, and once at night before sleep. These are the most powerful moments to imprint your subconscious mind.*
>
> — *The more deeply and intensely you visualize it with discipline every day, the sooner your miracle will manifest in your reality.*

Miracles happen, and anything can manifest because we are living in a Simulation. This reality is much like a virtual world or a video game, where there is always a possibility of applying a cheat code, or a glitch or defect in the software of the Divine Matrix. In this simulated experience, anything is possible.

Albert Einstein once said, "Everything is energy and that's all there is to it. Match the frequency of the energy you want, and you cannot help but get that reality. It can be no other way. This is not philosophy. This is physics."

Your ego-free, non-judgmental, and pure-loving Higher Self is always present, watching over you and gently guiding your journey. What may seem impossible from within the game can be effortlessly achieved by your Higher Self, Guardian Angels, or Divine Beings who exist outside the Simulation, where the limitations we perceive do not apply. To access their help, you must believe in them. Ask for their guidance and support with trust and openness.

Miracles are not bound by logic; they are born from faith, alignment, and connection with the unseen forces that are always with you.

Miracles don't follow logic.
They come from believing, being in tune with
yourself, and feeling connected to the invisible
forces that are always around you.

CHAPTER 10

Reasons Why Your Manifestation Isn't Working and How to Fix Them

There could be several reasons why your manifestations are not working. In this chapter, I will explain a few of them. It's important for you to take a careful look at your life to understand what might be causing your lack of success.

1. The 80/20 Rule of Manifestation

One of the most overlooked principles in manifestation is the 80/20 Rule. For any desire to manifest, 80% of the work must be done within your subconscious mind, primarily through repetition and visualization. The remaining 20% involves taking inspired action in the physical world. Once it is manifested in your subconscious mind, it will manifest in the physical reality. It's a universal law. If your manifestations aren't working, it's time to ask yourself, "Am I doing the 80% inner work?"

Take time each day to consciously visualize your goals and intentions. Follow the exercises mentioned in this book. Repeat them consistently to embed your intentions into your subconscious mind. When your inner world is aligned, the outer world follows effortlessly. Once your vision is clear and your energy is aligned, the 20% action becomes easy, natural, and often joyful.

2. **Raise Your Vibration to Align with Your Desires**

   If your manifestation isn't working, one key reason could be that your vibration is too low to match the frequency of your desired reality. When you're stuck in emotions like revenge, stress, frustration, anger, trauma, regret, or negativity. You're operating far below the frequency of love, abundance, peace, and calmness—the energies required for manifestation.

   To shift this, begin with self-love and forgiveness. Forgive yourself. Forgive others. Heal from past wounds not just mentally, but physically and emotionally as well. Seek therapy to process unresolved trauma. Release physical tension stored in the body through movement, breathwork, or somatic healing. Unblock your chakras through meditation, energy work, or spiritual practices. Nourish your body with healthy food, regular exercise, and rest. Travel, explore, and reconnect with life's beauty. Meditate daily to calm the mind and open the heart.

   Cheat Code to Manifest Miracles

Stop waiting for an external God or deity to come and forgive you. You have the power to forgive yourself. You are your own healer, your own guide, and your own miracle. When you raise your vibration, you align with the frequency of your desires, and that's when manifestation becomes effortless.

3. You Speak or Think Negatively About Yourself

One of the most powerful blocks to manifestation is negative self-talk. When you constantly speak or think poorly about yourself, even unconsciously, you lower your vibration and send conflicting signals to the Universe. Statements like

a. "I'm not good enough"
b. "Nothing ever works out for me"
c. "I always mess things up."

These thoughts become affirmations, and the Universe responds accordingly. To manifest your desires, you must become your own biggest supporter. Speak to yourself with kindness, compassion, and belief. Replace negative thoughts with empowering ones:

a. "I am worthy."
b. "I am capable."
c. "I am confident."
d. "I am blessed."
e. "I am worthy of all the love in the world."
f. "I am worthy of all the success, name and fame in the world."

Your words are spells and work like mantras. Your thoughts are energy. What you say to yourself becomes your reality.

4. You Don't Have a Burning Desire

If you don't have a burning desire or a clear intention to accomplish something, you may find yourself drifting, lacking passion, ambition, and the drive to achieve greater things. Without that inner fire, your goals remain distant, your actions inconsistent, and your focus is easily swayed by whatever new interest comes along. Remember, if you have a burning desire, it indicates that what you want has already manifested in the future, and if you take action toward it, engage in reverse engineering, and have complete certainty in your vision, you will be able to manifest it, no matter how much time and effort it requires.

A burning desire is more than just wanting something; it's the fuel that keeps you disciplined in your practices, whether it's meditation, visualization, decision-making, or taking bold action. Without it, your energy scatters, and your dreams fade into the background. To manifest anything meaningful, you must first identify what truly excites you. What stirs your soul? What goal would you pursue even if it seemed impossible?

Start by

   a. making a list of everything that sparks your interest

   b. review it often

c. notice which items consistently call to you; those are the ones aligned with your deeper purpose

d. choose the one that makes you feel like you could move mountains—and commit to it with your whole heart.

Your burning desire is your compass. Let it guide you, energize you, and remind you of the greatness you're capable of achieving.

5. You Don't Have a Crystal-Clear Picture of Your Desire or Goal

One of the most common reasons manifestations fail is a lack of clarity. If you don't know exactly what you want, how can the Universe deliver it? Vague intentions lead to ambiguous results. When your desire is unclear, your energy becomes scattered, and your subconscious mind doesn't know what to focus on. To manifest effectively, you must create a crystal-clear mental image of your goal or outcome. Ask yourself,

a. "What exactly do I want?"

b. "What does it look like, feel like, sound like?"

c. "How will I know when I've achieved it?"

The more specific and emotionally charged your vision, the more powerfully it will imprint on your subconscious mind, and the faster it will begin to manifest in your reality. Clarity is magnetic. When you are clear, the Universe responds with precision.

6. You're Too Attached to the Outcome

One major block to manifestation is over-focusing on the outcome and obsessing over how it should happen. When you're overly attached or clingy to the result, you create resistance in your energy field. Always remember, you can only take action and give your absolute best; the outcome is never in your control. The more you try to control the outcome, the more it will slip away from your hands.

Constantly thinking, "When will it happen?" "Why hasn't it happened yet?" or "I've meditated and visualized, why isn't it manifesting?" only delays the process. Understand that good things often take time, especially in this Simulation where we are bound by space and time. Your role is to do the inner and outer work, release the desire, and then maintain your inner peace, vibration, and frequency. Trust the process. Believe that your desire has already manifested in the future, and that's why you have this burning desire in your heart in the present. Let go of control and allow the Universe to deliver it in the best possible way.

7. You Don't Believe in Miracles; You Only Believe in Yourself

Another reason your manifestations may not be working is that you've placed all your faith solely in yourself, and none in the Creator, the Universe, or the Divine Intelligence that orchestrates all things. Miracles are not logical; they are Divine alignments that occur when you surrender control and trust in something greater than yourself. You must believe that the Universe is working with you, not against you.

You need to understand that the Creator wants to bless you, not punish you. No matter your past or your actions, you are always loved by the Creator. He is not sitting anywhere waiting for an opportunity to punish you, and there is no such thing as hell or heaven. Instead, you have the power to create your own hell and heaven through your mind's power while navigating this Matrix. Open your heart to the possibility that you are not alone. You are guided. You are supported. And yes, miracles are real.

8. You're Not Visualizing in the Present Moment (NOW)

One of the most common mistakes in manifestation is visualizing your desires as something that will happen someday, in the future. But manifestation doesn't respond to "someday." It responds to now. When you visualize your desire, you must do it as if it's already happening in this very moment.

Feel it. See it. Live it in the now. Now, the present moment is all we have. If you keep thinking, "I will have it soon," or "It's coming," you're energetically placing your desire in the future, and that's exactly where it will stay.

To manifest powerfully,

a. visualize your goal as already achieved

b. feel the emotions of joy, gratitude, and fulfilment in the present moment

c. speak in the present tense: "I am," not "I will be."

The subconscious mind doesn't distinguish between imagination and reality; it responds to emotion and presence. So, the more real it feels, the faster it becomes your reality.

9. You Don't Believe in Yourself or Your Worthiness

Another major block to manifestation is self-doubt. You may not believe in your own abilities. You may carry a limited belief system that tells you you're not capable, not worthy, or not deserving of the life you desire. This often leads to self-sabotage. When opportunities arise, you might unconsciously push them away or make choices that reinforce your belief that "this can't be real" or "I don't deserve this" or "no one in my family ever done this" or "too much money is evil" or "wealthy people are not happy" or "big project or big team will increase my stress."

Or you may be stuck in a lack mindset, constantly feeling like there's not enough; not enough time, money, love, or support. And when you don't believe you're worthy, you energetically block the very things you're trying to attract.

Imagine you're like a 10-watt bulb, but your dreams and goals need 1,000 watts of energy to shine. To manifest that kind of power, you first need to grow—mentally, emotionally, and spiritually. This means investing in yourself, building your skills, and expanding your inner capacity to hold more light. If you try to hold more energy than you're ready for, you might "short-circuit"—feel overwhelmed, stuck, or engage in self-sabotage. But when you're prepared, you can not only attract what you desire but also sustain it with confidence and grace.

To overcome doubts and feelings of unworthiness, use the affirmations and mantras we discussed earlier. They help you rewire your mindset and remind you that you are worthy of everything you wish to create.

10. You're Afraid of What Happens if it Comes True

Sometimes, the biggest block to manifestation is not failure, it's the fear of success. You may consciously desire something like a relationship, a marriage, a dream job, but deep down, you're afraid of what will happen if it actually comes true. This creates an energetic contradiction: Your conscious mind says yes, but your subconscious says no.

You might think,

    a. "What if I'm not ready?"

    b. "What if I lose it?"

    c. "What if it changes everything?"

This fear leads to self-sabotage, hesitation, or mixed signals to the Universe. You may unknowingly push away the very thing you're trying to attract. To overcome this,

    a. acknowledge your fears without judgment

    b. journal about what you're afraid might happen if your desire manifests

    c. visualize yourself handling success with grace, confidence, and joy

    d. repeat, "I am safe to receive what I desire."

You are not just worthy of your dreams; you are capable of living them fully.

11. You're Living in Past Trauma, Regret, or Loss

If you find yourself stuck in the past, replaying trauma, regret, or grief, it can block your ability to manifest and move forward. These emotional wounds create energetic patterns that keep you anchored in pain, preventing you from stepping into your power. Instead of asking, "Why is this happening to me?" shift your perspective to

    a. "What is this trying to teach me?"

    b. "Why did my soul choose this experience?"

    c. "What did I come here to learn?"

This shift transforms suffering into wisdom. It allows you to see your life as a soul's journey, a Divine curriculum designed for growth, healing, and awakening. Every challenge holds a lesson. Every loss carries a deeper truth. When you begin to heal and release the past, you create space for miracles to enter.

12. You're Jealous of Others' Success and Secretly Wish Them to Fail

Jealousy is a powerful energy, but not in a good way. When you envy others or secretly wish for their downfall, you create a low vibration of lack, resentment, anger, and separation. This energy not only blocks your own manifestations but also attracts similar experiences into your life.

Judging others based on their looks, circumstances, or achievements sends a message to the Universe: "I don't believe there's enough for everyone, including me." But here's the truth: Whatever you judge, you will eventually face. Life mirrors your inner world. If you project negativity, you will experience it. If you celebrate others, you open the door for your own blessings.

To shift this, practice genuine appreciation for others' success.

a. Repeat, "If it's possible for them, it's possible for me."

b. Heal the parts of you that feel unworthy or left behind.

c. Replace judgment with curiosity and compassion.

The Universe is abundant. The sun shines equally on everyone. There's more than enough for everyone.

When you celebrate others, you align with the energy of receiving, and your own miracles begin to unfold.

13. You're Entangling Yourself in Other People's Karma Through Gossip and Negativity

One of the most subtle yet powerful blocks to manifestation is getting involved in other people's lives through gossip, judgment, or negative talk. When you speak negatively about others, you energetically entangle yourself in their karmic patterns, and this can severely hinder your own spiritual and manifestation progress.

It's none of your business who others are with, what they're doing, or how they're living. Every time you speak a negative word, you create a ripple of energy that returns to you. This is the Law of Cause and Effect, and it is always in motion. Gossip and judgment don't just affect your energy; they affect your

a. health

b. personality

c. perception of reality

d. even your DNA.

Too much negativity increases suffering, clouds your intuition, and lowers your vibration. It keeps you emotionally entangled in stories that aren't yours to carry. To protect your peace and power,

a. mind your own energy

b. limit unnecessary social engagement

c. avoid gossip and drama

d. choose silence over judgment

e. live a life of emotional detachment and inner clarity.

Not knowing others' stories, affairs, or personal lives is a form of spiritual freedom. Stay in your lane. Protect your frequency. Manifest your goals in peace. Always remember that every action has a reaction; negative actions or gossip will bring similar negativity back to you.

14. You're Too Focused on Making Money Instead of Serving Others

When your primary focus is on making money, rather than providing value or service, you disconnect from the true flow of abundance. Money is not the goal; it's a byproduct of the energy you offer. The Universe responds to intention and alignment. When you serve others with love, purpose, and authenticity, money flows naturally as an energy exchange, not as something to chase or control. Being overly cautious, fearful, or stingy with money indicates a mindset focused on lack, poverty, and scarcity. Remember, money is just energy. It flows where there is trust, generosity, and openness. If you constantly worry about spending, hoarding resources, or fear losing what you have, you block the natural flow of abundance. Instead, practice.

a. gratitude for what you have

b. generosity in giving

c. trust in receiving.

Money is not your master; it's your mirror. When you shift your relationship with it, you shift your entire reality. Your manifestation should come from a higher purpose, not just from ego or personal desire. If you desire fame, ask yourself what you will do with that power once it manifests. The feeling of serving others should be the prime objective of any manifestation.

15. You're Not Following Your Passion

One of the most powerful ways to align with your highest potential is to follow your passion. Your soul came here with a purpose. Don't silence it. When you ignore your creativity and what lights you up and your natural gifts, interests, and soul-driven desires, you disconnect from your true path and your soul mission, and you ignore signals and guidance given by your Higher Self. This blocks the connection with the Divine energies and flow of abundance and fulfilment.

I'm not saying that following your passion will be free of challenges. The purpose of a simulator is to guide you through experiences and challenges—so you can learn, grow, and evolve from them. Therefore, challenges, struggles, and obstacles are part of the journey, but they exist to help you grow and evolve as a soul. Through these experiences, you become more accomplished and aligned with your higher purpose, and you are always supported by the Universe. Face your challenges with curiosity, not fear. Reflect on how your passion can serve you, and more importantly, how it can serve others.

    Cheat Code to Manifest Miracles

When you align your purpose with service, you will be supported by the Divine and your spirit guides. You'll begin to notice positive synchronicities unfolding in your life, guiding and supporting your journey. Passion, creativity, love, and curiosity are some of the ways our Higher Self and the Universe communicate with us. If you do not follow your passions, the Universe may stop guiding you until you take action on your passion. Step out of your comfort zone, be creative and act on your passion now.

Your passion is not random. It's a Divine compass guiding you toward your soul's purpose. When you align with your true path, synchronicities unfold effortlessly. The right people, situations, connections, and opportunities will appear, as if by magic—all orchestrated to support your soul's mission. The key is to raise your frequency and follow your passion wholeheartedly, without compromising your energetic alignment. Stay elevated. Stay true to your mission. The Universe will respond to your vision.

Your creativity is your power to create in this Simulation and become the co-creator of your destiny. When you do what you love, you raise your vibration, attract aligned opportunities, and feel energized instead of drained. If you're only doing what's "safe" or "expected," ask yourself,

a. "What brings me joy, even if no one pays me for it?"
b. "What would I like to do if there were no time and money constraints?"
c. "What do I lose track of time doing?"

d. "What did I love as a child before the world told me who to be?"

Following your passion doesn't require you to quit everything overnight. It means honoring your inner calling in small ways each day. If you can't follow your passion as a full-time career, consider pursuing it as a hobby or a part-time endeavor on weekends. Ultimately, it's up to you how you follow your passion, when you choose to act on it, and at what pace you move forward. The path is yours to shape.

16. You're Neglecting Your Well-being, Health, and Fitness

Your body is the temple of your soul, and if you're not taking care of it, you're weakening the foundation of your manifestation power. When you consume too much junk food, fast food, processed food, alcohol, sugar, or meat (especially from sources that carry trauma in their DNA), you lower your vibration and disrupt your energetic balance. These foods can dull your intuition, cloud your mind, and create emotional and physical imbalances that block your spiritual growth. Neglecting your health sends a message to the Universe: "I'm not ready to receive."

To realign,

a. **eat high-vibrational foods** – fresh fruits, vegetables, whole grains, and clean water

b. **move your body** – through yoga, breathing exercise, core and strength training, cardio, walking, dancing, or any form of joyful exercise

c. **rest and recharge** – your nervous system needs peace to stay in alignment; rest plenty

d. **detox your body and mind** – reduce toxins, both physical and emotional.

When you prioritize your well-being, you raise your frequency, and that's when miracles begin to flow.

17. You're Surrounding Yourself with the Wrong People

Your environment shapes your energy, and your energy shapes your reality. If you're spending time with people who don't believe in you, who mock your dreams, or who secretly want you to fail, you're sabotaging your own growth. These people may

a. constantly emit negative energy

b. dismiss your ideas as "stupid" or "unrealistic"

c. undermine your confidence

d. play the victim and pull you into their drama

e. be jealous of your potential and try to keep you small.

And the hardest truth? These people may be in your own household, inner circle, or even your family. You must learn to disconnect with such people, not with hate, but with clarity. You can still love them, check in occasionally, and wish them well, but you don't have to let them influence your energy or decisions.

Stop living your life for others. Live your own life. Prioritize your goals. Protect your peace. Remember, negativity is contagious, like a virus. It spreads quickly and pulls you down before you even realize it. You must be intentional about who you allow into your energetic space. Even well-meaning people, including parents, may not be the right ones to advise you on your career, finances, or dreams. Take advice only from those who are living the life you aspire to. Surround yourself with people who

a. inspire you

b. support your growth

c. celebrate your wins

d. challenge you to rise higher.

Your circle matters. Choose it wisely.

18. You're Not Open-Minded or Mindful; So, You Miss Opportunities

Manifestation requires more than just desire; it requires alertness, mindfulness, and awareness. If you're not open-minded or present in the moment, you may fail to recognize the very opportunities, people, or signs that are meant to guide you toward your goals.

When your mind is closed, distracted, or rigid in its expectations, you

a. overlook Divine timing

b. miss out on connections that could elevate your journey

c. dismiss ideas or people that don't fit your limited view

d. stay stuck in old patterns while new doors quietly open and close.

Every opportunity has a window. And that window doesn't stay open forever. To align with your manifestations,

a. practice mindfulness — be fully present in your daily life

b. stay open to new ideas, people, and paths

c. trust that the Universe may deliver your desire in unexpected ways

d. let go of rigid expectations and allow space for magic.

The Universe is always speaking, but you must be calm, still, open, and aware enough to listen. Pay attention to Divine signals, omens, dreams, messages that may come through your friends, strangers, phone calls, billboards, etc.

19. You Find Problems in Every Solution and Live in Complaint Mode

Stop seeing yourself as a victim in every situation. If you're constantly finding flaws, complaining about everything, or playing the victim in every situation, you're unknowingly blocking your own growth and manifestations. This mindset creates a cycle of

a. negativity

b. blame

c. powerlessness.

When you focus on what's wrong instead of what's possible, you train your mind to expect disappointment. You become blind to solutions, opportunities, and blessings, even when they're right in front of you. Victimhood may feel safe. It might even bring temporary attention or sympathy from friends, placing you in the spotlight for a while. But it keeps you stuck. It convinces you that life is happening to you, not for you. Eventually, smart and successful people will begin to distance themselves, and you'll only attract those who mirror your low frequency and victimhood mindset. Like energy attracts like energy—and if you stay stuck, so will your circle.

To shift this,

a. practice gratitude daily, even for small things

b. replace complaints with constructive action

c. ask, "What can I learn from this?" instead of "Why me?"

d. take complete responsibility for your energy and choices.

You are not powerless. You are powerful. But that power only activates when you stop complaining and start creating.

20. You Are Not Protecting Your Manifestation Energy

One of the most common mistakes in the manifestation journey is disclosing your plans too early. When inspiration strikes and a vision begins to form, it's natural to feel excited and want to share it with others. But this impulse can be energetically risky.

Not everyone will celebrate your dreams. Some may consciously or unconsciously project doubt, envy, or negativity toward your plans. These subtle energetic influences—whether spoken or felt—can interfere with your manifestation process. Everything is energy. Thoughts carry vibrations. When someone doubts your vision or secretly wishes for your failure, that energy can create resistance in your field, blocking the flow of your manifestation.

Make this your thumb rule:

a. until your plans are concrete and the planning phase is complete, do not disclose your manifestation journey to anyone who doesn't need to know.

b. keep your vision sacred. Work silently. Let your results speak.

c. people cannot affect what they do not know about. The less exposed your dreams are to external energies, the more protected and potent they remain. This is not secrecy out of fear—it is sacred silence out of wisdom.

d. avoid environments where you feel pressured to explain your journey—parties, social gatherings, or conversations that demand updates. These spaces often dilute your focus and invite unnecessary energetic interference. Instead, choose solitude, intentional action, and inner alignment.

e. limit social media sharing. Avoid posting about your goals or early-stage plans online. Share only after manifestation has occurred or when the energy is stable.

f. set boundaries in conversations: if someone asks about your plans, gently redirect the conversation or say, "I'm working on something special—I'll share it when the time is right."

g. celebrate quiet wins: acknowledge your progress privately. You don't need external validation. Your soul knows the truth of your journey.

21. You Are Not Spiritual

You may not consider yourself a spiritual person. Perhaps you don't believe in a Higher Power or Divine Intelligence that can bring miracles into your life. You might believe that everything is limited to the here and now, and that you are just a human being, and there's nothing beyond or above you. But spirituality isn't about following a specific religion or adhering to rigid protocol.

Spirituality is about opening yourself to the possibility that there is something greater—a force of unconditional love, wisdom, and intelligence that exists beyond what we can see or measure. Believing in a higher power doesn't mean abandoning logic; it means expanding your perspective. It allows you to see

Cheat Code to Manifest Miracles

beyond your limitations, to trust in the unseen, and to invite miracles into your life. When you align with this greater energy, life begins to unfold in ways that feel guided, purposeful, and deeply connected.

FINAL REFLECTION: YOU ARE THE MIRACLE

Throughout history, across all faiths and religions, we have witnessed Ascended Masters perform miracles — not as magic tricks, but as divine expressions of truth. How?

- *They practiced Stillness, lived in Awareness, and remained Non-reactive.*
- *They held Unshakable Faith — not hope, but Complete Certainty.*
- *They were deeply united with the Source, the Divine Consciousness, knowing this world is Maya, an illusion — a Divine Matrix.*
- *They faced tests and challenges with Grace, knowing the soul is here to Evolve.*
- *They understood the Creative Power of Thoughts and Emotions.*
- *Their miracles came from Pure Intent, Compassion, and Unconditional Love in service to humanity.*
- *They were aligned with Natural and Spiritual Laws.*
- *Miracles weren't exceptions — they were expressions of*

Higher Truths.

They didn't just believe in miracles — they became the Miracle.

Now, it's your turn.

- *Be Still.*
- *Be Non-reactive.*
- *Be Aware.*
- *Be Present.*
- *Be Authentic.*
- *Believe with Certainty.*
- *Understand the Power of Your Thoughts and Emotions.*
- *Align with Unconditional Love.*

And remember — the power that moved through them, moves through you.

 *You are the Miracle. You always were.* 

Take a quiet moment and ask yourself: **"What miracle am I ready to embody today?"**

Let this question guide your next step — not from fear, but from faith and certainty. Your journey begins now.

IndiePress

The best route your story can take.

To publish your own book, contact us.

We publish poetry collections, short story collections, novellas and novels.

contact@http://indiepress.in/

Instagram- indie_press